CAS TIGERS

The Breakthrough Year!

League Publications Ltd

Foreword by Martyn Sadler, Editor, League Express

By Callum Walker

First published in Great Britain in 2017 by
League Publications Ltd, Wellington House, Briggate,
Brighouse, West Yorkshire HD6 1DN

A CIP catalogue record for this book is available from the British Library

ISBN 978-1-901347-35-7

Designed and Typeset by League Publications Limited
Printed by H Charlesworth & Co Ltd, Wakefield

Editing and Design
Alex Davis

Photography
Matthew Merrick

Additional Photography
Brian King
Richard Land
David Murgatroyd
NRL Imagery
RL Photos
Thinkstock
UK Sports Pics Ltd

Contents

Thank you to my mother, Julie Walker, as I wouldn't be where I am today without her advice, guidance and continuous support. I would also like to thank my late grandfather, Ronald Stather, a truly genuine and thoughtful person whose morals have influenced me ever since.

Foreword

by Martyn Sadler,
Editor, League Express

Castleford Tigers created history in 2017, finishing at the top of the league for the first time in the club's 91-year history, winning the League Leaders' Shield and finishing ten points ahead of Leeds Rhinos, their nearest challengers, at the end of the Super 8s.

But it wasn't just history the Tigers created in 2017.

It was jet-heeled excitement and an astonishing feelgood factor that swept everybody in Rugby League along with it.

For example, in only their second game of the season they travelled to the Halliwell Jones Stadium to play Warrington Wolves, who had beaten Brisbane Broncos the previous weekend in one of the most impressive wins we have seen by a Super League club against NRL opposition. The Wolves were being talked up as potential Super League Champions.

And yet in a spell of sustained brilliance the Tigers blitzed them with a four-try burst in the first half that was just unstoppable, causing me to wax lyrical about the Tigers in that week's edition of League Express, while making quite an extravagant comparison.

"On Friday night Castleford Tigers served us up nine minutes of almost perfect Rugby League, during which time they scored four scintillating tries," I wrote.

"It was almost certainly the most astonishing nine minutes of action that I can recall watching.

"It actually took me back to the brilliance of the 1982 Australian tourists, who were also capable of unleashing a barrage of tries against unsuspecting opponents in a very short space of time.

"It was a privilege to see it, and there's no doubt in my mind that if the Tigers could sustain rugby like that for long periods throughout a game, then they would be almost unbeatable."

The funny thing was that Castleford's performance was not originally scheduled to be captured by the TV cameras, which should have been at Wigan for their game against Widnes. But Wigan postponed that game because of bad weather affecting the pitch at the DW Stadium and the Sky cameras had to head to Warrington at short notice.

Thank goodness they did, as I also wrote in that League Express column.

"After the Wigan postponement debacle last week I joked on Twitter that anyone looking for a conspiracy theory about why Wigan had called off their game should look to Sky Sports, who had been due to broadcast the clash between Wigan and Widnes, but must have been looking enviously earlier in the week at the clash between Warrington and

Castleford, which always looked like the obvious game to broadcast," I said.

"Whatever the rights and wrongs of Wigan postponing their game, and then rearranging it, the truth is that Sky viewers were all fortunate that Sky switched to the Halliwell Jones Stadium."

Sky continued to follow Castleford around the Betfred Super League as the season unfolded, and we saw many memorable games and superb performances, both from the team and from individuals within it.

It was a season that I will always remember and I'm sure that every Castleford supporter will feel the same way.

That's why we commissioned Callum Walker, himself a Castleford supporter, to write a book that would document what is perhaps the most successful season in the club's history.

It may have ended in heartbreak at Old Trafford with a Grand Final defeat to Leeds Rhinos, but that shouldn't be allowed to cloud our view of what was a wonderful Rugby League season, with Castleford giving us truly a season to remember.

I hope you all enjoy re-living the 2017 season as much as I have.

Introduction

In the Chinese calendar, 2017 is the Year of the Rooster. According to traditional Chinese zodiac analysis, the Rooster is the representative of confidence and intelligence whilst people born in the Years of the Rooster are said to possess characteristics such as being responsive, distinctive, smart and intensely committed.

Translate this on to the Rugby League field and the Castleford Tigers have displayed all the traits befitting the Chinese Year of the Rooster. Hopeful optimism amongst fans and players alike in pre-season quickly developed into expectancy as February and March passed, with the Tigers brushing away most of their competitors in exhilarating fashion, notching up seriously impressive wins, more often than not with blow-out scores, and against some of the league's best. Fourth, and two fifth-placed finishes in the three seasons prior to 2017, makes the Tigers' astonishing season appear as if it has materialised 'out of the blue'.

But this is a rise that has been brewing for years. In 2013, Steve Gill, the former scoreboard operator turned head of youth and lifelong Castleford fan, was surprisingly promoted to the role of chief executive, following the high-profile departure of the controversial Steve Ferres. Gill had an immense task to stop the stagnation that had long set in at the club and turn around the club's fortunes. Fortunes which in 2014, forced the club to sell one of their most prized and coveted assets, Daryl Clark, to Warrington just to stay afloat. When Gill took over, off-field problems were in abundance and with administration looming and performances on the field suffering alongside, just three points from a possible 22 in the Tigers' opening 11 games of the 2013 season, the future looked increasingly bleak for the historically-rich club.

Enter Daryl Powell. Taking the reins from Danny Orr, who filled in for three games as coach, after Ian Millward had been sacked following a dismal run of form that had seen home crowds dwindle to less than 4,000 spectators. The former Featherstone Rovers boss made inroads as soon as he arrived. With Danny Orr and Ryan Sheridan as his assistants, the latter following Powell from Featherstone Rovers, the backroom picture was injected with experience and talent. A remarkable 49-24 victory over arch-rivals Wakefield Trinity Wildcats (as they were known then) was such evidence of the impact Powell and his assistants was starting to make. A twelfth-placed finish was not to be sneered at considering the Tigers had been languishing at the foot of the table for most of the season.

A Wembley visit and fourth position beckoned in 2014 whilst two fifth-placed finishes

in 2015 and 2016 were a sign of the consistency necessary for Castleford to consolidate themselves as a top-four side.

Then, 2017 appeared. The media hype before February brought a pressure upon the West Yorkshire outfit rarely experienced in this "small town in Wakefield", as the Castleford fans call themselves to mock their rivals from much larger towns or cities. Fast-flowing, exciting and at times, flamboyant Rugby League has endeared the Tigers to the Rugby League fraternity as a whole, with pundits and even the RFL waxing lyrical about "Classy Cas", a phrase first coined in the 1960s to describe the free-flowing brand of rugby under then coach, George Clinton.

Under Powell, the class has been well and truly put back into Cas. "Good times never seemed so good," a line from the Tigers' adopted victory song, Sweet Caroline, a regular feature belted out at full-time around the Mend-a-Hose Jungle in 2017, describes perfectly the emotion the Castleford supporters experienced throughout 2017.

After 91 years of failing to ever finish the season top of the table, 23 years without any major silverware, and the misery endured in the decade before Powell's tenure, the loyal fans of Castleford could scarcely believe what they witnessed in 2017. This book is a celebration of this quite unbelievable breakthrough year for the Tigers and their long-suffering fans.

Callum Walker

DENNY SOLOMONA SAGA

AS REPORTED BY LEAGUE EXPRESS

SOLOMONA CLOSE TO JOINING SHARKS

Castleford Tigers winger Denny Solomona, according to the League Express, was said to be close to joining Rugby Union side Sale Sharks.

Solomona, who broke Super League's try-scoring record following a 40-try haul in 2016, was rumoured to be on the verge of a code-switch in a deal thought to be in the region of £350,000.

Gloucester RU were also thought to be chasing the Samoan international, however, Sale were the ones who had appeared to have coaxed Solomona to leave Rugby League for the 15-man game, a game he played as a youngster.

Speculation surrounding the ex-London winger had never been far away from the headlines. He had been previously linked with a move to Wigan Warriors following the news of Josh Charnley's departure, who also joined Sale at the end of the 2016 season, while he was then rumoured to be on his way to Warrington as part of a big money move.

However, reports linking him with a Rugby Union switch were also rife, with Gloucester's interest emerging in September 2016.

25th October 2016

STEVE GILL DENIES SOLOMONA SALE

Castleford Tigers chairman Steve Gill publicly denied that the club had sold winger Denny Solomona and that he was not for sale at any cost.

Gill was defiant in the unfolding situation: "We have rebuffed three approaches for Denny, two from Rugby Union and one from Rugby League. He is not for sale," Gill told BBC Radio Leeds.

"We haven't sold him and we're not loaning him back like I've heard from some rumours.

"We expect Denny back in training on 7 November with the rest of the squad."

RFL BACKS THE TIGERS

Castleford Tigers received the support of the Rugby Football League (RFL) in their fight against Denny Solomona's impending exit from the club, and the sport.

Solomona's cross-code transfer to Sale Sharks was expected to be announced by the Rugby Union side later in November.

But Castleford remained defiant in their claims that they had not agreed to sell Solomona and that the deal had moved forward without their consent. The Tigers also sought out the RFL for guidance about how to handle the situation.

Sale were reportedly intent on stressing Solomona had no Rugby Union contract, therefore a transfer fee was not necessary. However, Castleford stood their ground, demanding that they were owed a fee whilst also emphasising that they had not formally agreed to sell the winger.

It was thought that this dispute could result in a high-profile legal battle should the Sharks announce the deal without Castleford's consent. The RFL meanwhile, came out in public support for the Tigers in a case that could have had massive repercussions for both sports.

League Express also reported that Solomona's management were being investigated by the RFL, with the handling of the Solomona transfer the focal point of the investigation.

21st November 2016

TIGERS STILL IN DARK

Castleford Tigers were still in the dark with regards to the Denny Solomona situation.

The club had not commented publicly on the matter since November 8, in which they confirmed they had "instructed their lawyers" after the winger posted a video on social media site Instagram, which appeared to show him with a number of Sale players. Solomona had not attended any of Castleford's pre-season training up to this point, while an incriminating picture had emerged of a Sale Sharks van allegedly parked outside his house.

Whilst Sale were still adamant that they did not owe Castleford a transfer fee as Solomona had no Rugby Union contract,

Castleford still insisted that a fee was required and again reiterated that they had not agreed to sell the winger.

24th November 2016

CAS GO TO COURT

Castleford Tigers announced that they would be taking legal action against Denny Solomona for his failure to show up for pre-season training.

TIGERS RAMP UP LEGAL ACTION

Castleford Tigers stepped up their efforts to launch legal proceedings against winger Denny Solomona as both sides refused to give the other an inch over the dispute.

Solomona had still not been present at the Mend-A-Hose Jungle ahead of his widely-expected cross-code switch to Sale.

League Express also reported that Solomona had been training with Sale for a number of weeks ahead of the future announcement from the Rugby Union side that Super League's top try-scorer was a Sale player with immediate effect.

The Tigers, in the week before, had started pre-action claims with their legal team, which included sports barrister Richard Cramer and the renowned Nick Randall QC, whose clients include the England football captain, Wayne Rooney.

The West Yorkshire club believed that they had enough evidence to build a case against both the winger and Sale. But the two would be separate cases, with the battle against Solomona the main issue as things stood, with Sale not directly involved up to this point.

League Express also reported earlier in November 2016 that the Rugby Football League had given Castleford their full backing in their bid to seek legal action over the winger after he failed to return to the club as agreed.

Sources close to the RFL indicated to League Express that the situation had not changed, and with Castleford set to go to the High Court, the battle between the parties was becoming progressively uglier.

It was also claimed that Solomona had reportedly resigned to try and push through his move to Rugby Union and the Sharks, something Castleford rightly refused to accept.

The 'retirement' claim meant that Sale could then technically acquire the player for nothing with the argument that he had retired as a Rugby League player and was not under contract with any sporting club.

Meanwhile, the RFL had spoken with Solomona's management as part of the investigation into his conduct the week before.

League Express revealed exclusively earlier in November that Andy Clarke, Solomona's agent, was set to be the subject of an investigation, and it was understood that the RFL would decide in the following week whether they would charge him over any misconduct. On the same day, Director of Rugby of Sale Sharks, Steve Diamond, told BBC Sport that "Denny Solomona has resigned from playing Rugby League and us, and many other clubs, are interested in signing him."

"He's got a friendship with [Sale centre] Sam Tuitupou and he's been to have a look around and at this moment that is where we're at with it."

"There are no governing body registrations between the sports," added Diamond.

"It is just like someone coming from another sport to Rugby Union, whether it be football or basketball and I don't understand what the furore is about."

Clearly, Diamond and Sale Sharks, believed they had done absolutely nothing wrong in their pursuit of the record-breaker Solomona.

5th December 2016

SOLOMONA HANDED WORK PERMIT

There was yet another significant step forward in Denny Solomona's impending exit from Castleford Tigers, with the winger being granted a work permit as his potential cross-code switch to Rugby Union side Sale Sharks neared ever closer.

Solomona had informed Castleford he had 'retired' from Rugby League with immediate effect shortly after failing to report for pre-season training in November. At the same time, it was evident that he had been training with the Sharks for a number of weeks as a move to the 15-man code loomed large on the horizon.

League Express also reported that the Rugby Football League, as part of their decision to support Castleford throughout the transfer saga, sought out the Rugby Football Union to try and reach an amicable conclusion to the situation.

However, their attempts to resolve the matter fell on deaf ears, as did their attempts to speak to Premiership Rugby, the governing body which oversees the top tier of domestic Rugby Union in the UK. Neither Sale nor the RFU therefore believed that the Sharks had done any wrong in their incessant pursuit of record-breaker Solomona, a worrying development for Rugby League as a whole.

At this point Castleford's legal team, including the renowned barrister Nick Randall QC, were waiting for Sale to announce the signing of the 23-year-old before they determined their next move.

RFU SPEAKS OUT

The Rugby Football Union spoke for the first time regarding Sale's signing of Denny Solomona. The RFU stated that they respected the RFL's concerns regarding the "sanctity of contracts" but that the RFU did not have the jurisdiction to act.

"The employment status with a club in a different sport is a matter between that club and the player," an RFU spokesman told BBC Sport.

Just three days before, the RFU had refuted the RFL's attempts to find some kind of settlement, now they had basically given Sale the green light for the controversial move to go ahead.

13th December 2016

CAS ISSUE LEGAL PAPERS TO SOLOMONA

Castleford Tigers served legal papers on their former player Denny Solomona, after Sale Sharks registered Solomona to play in the 2017 European Champions Cup Rugby Union competition last week.

It was the first time that the Sharks had taken any step that suggested they had agreed a contract with Solomona, who had walked out of the Tigers with two years remaining on his contract at the Mend-a-Hose Jungle.

League Express also understood that the Sharks had to comply with a registration deadline if Solomona was to be eligible for any games in that competition in 2017.

The club had however not yet registered him to play in the Aviva Premiership.

The Sharks didn't select Solomona for their Champions Cup clash against Saracens the preceding Saturday. However, the Rugby Union club did announce Solomona's signature just a few hours before the Tigers broadcasted that they would be taking the matter to court on the 13th.

On the confirmation, Steve Diamond, the Sale director of rugby, spoke in admiration of Solomona: "He is a great player.

"He has an eye for scoring tries and has the added bonus of having played Rugby Union in his time at school and college."

Meanwhile, the RFL Chief Executive, Nigel Wood, said that Solomona joining Sale would be hugely worrying for their sport. "This has profound implications for the game. Clearly the sanctity of contracts have to be respected. It's a concern for more than the game, it's bigger than just Rugby League or Rugby Union, it's almost like a law of the land issue really.

"As we have previously stated, the RFL believes that it is a fundamental point of principle for all sports that both players and clubs adhere to the terms of signed contracts between them.

"It is therefore not surprising that when a club believes the terms of a contract have been broken, they may issue legal proceedings to protect their position."

TIGERS DEMAND £500,000 IN DAMAGES

League Express reported that the Tigers were seeking £500,000 in what Castleford Tigers' Chief Executive, Steve Gill described as "damages and exemplary damages".

Steve Gill insisted that the issuing of legal proceedings against Sale Sharks, Denny Solomona and the former Tigers star's agent, Andy Clarke, was a last resort.

Castleford officials issued proceedings out of the High Court in Leeds, after the Sharks confirmed the week before that Solomona had penned a three-year deal to become a Rugby Union player.

He was then selected by the Sharks for the upcoming European Champions Cup game against Saracens at the A J Bell Stadium.

Gill again reiterated a strong response to the brass of Sale in their lengthy hunt for Solomona.

"We have lost a quality player who scored 42 tries last season and broke the Super League try-scoring record in the 2016 season," said Gill.

"In August, this year, we made it very clear to Solomona and Sale Sharks that there was an unbreakable contract in place until the end of season 2018, with no basis whatsoever for either ourselves or Solomona to depart from each other's mutual obligations.

"The idea of losing the player was not welcomed by us and we have repeatedly told Sale Sharks that it would be impermissible for them to talk to Solomona, let alone sign him. Clear unequivocal warnings have clearly been disregarded.

"The proceedings have been issued as a last resort, as we have failed over the last couple of weeks to try and resolve matters without the formality of court proceedings.

"We have confidence that the legal system will bring out all of the facts and the truth.

"We are fighting this not just for Castleford Tigers but also for the integrity of all sports, including of course Rugby Union clubs. Our belief is that all contracts are sacrosanct in professional and amateur sports."

Greg Mulholland, the MP for Leeds North West and the Chairman of the All-Party Parliamentary Rugby League Group also stepped in and called the actions of Solomona and Sale "disgraceful".

Mulholland added: "In the era of open rugby, there will, of course, be players who will, entirely reasonably, choose to play both codes.

"However, this must be done properly, as it has to when players change clubs within the same code. The blatant disregard that Sale Sharks and the player have shown for his existing contract must not be allowed to stand.

"To walk out of a legal contract and to sign a player in this position is completely unacceptable, as contracts must be honoured.

"The Group feels strongly that a player should not be able to walk away from a fixed contract without consequence, and is fully supportive of the stance the Rugby Football League has taken in this regard."

Former Bradford Bulls Chairman Peter Hood, who was heavily involved in his former club's case with Leeds Rhinos, concerning Iestyn Harris, believed that the Tigers had grounds for optimism in terms of securing damages for future losses as a result of Solomona's departure, in addition to the hindrance of not only sourcing his replacement but also attempting to succeed in his absence.

Hood said: "I'd expect Castleford to claim losses, for example, including profit on shirt sales, sponsorships, attendances and memberships in addition to the loss of the player's services on and off the field, their inability to adequately replace him and consequently their ability to win prize money and maybe trophies now being much reduced, plus reputational damage.

"For Bradford, with Harris, it boiled down to: do we take the 'litigation risk' and maybe win, recovering most of our costs in the process, or lose and face damages, paying the costs of the other side plus our own costs with no means of paying (within 14 days).

"So I settled, with time to pay the agreed sum, and drew a line under mounting legal bills. We lived to fight another day you might say.

"Perhaps though, and with 20/20 hindsight, it might have been better to go to trial. If we'd won, great!

"If not, it would have been Leeds that put Bradford out of business, but to the detriment of the game as a whole, one might argue."

20th December 2016

DIAMOND ISSUES CLAIMS

Sale Sharks' Director of Rugby, Steve Diamond, added yet another twist to the Denny Solomona saga by claiming that the winger had been fired by Castleford Tigers before the Sharks stepped in and signed him.

Diamond once again maintained that the Sharks had done nothing wrong in their pursuit of the 23-year-old, and now said that Castleford sacked their prized asset, a bizarre contradiction to Diamond's claim that Solomona had resigned.

"It's in the hands of the legal people, but I don't see any problems at this moment," Diamond told BBC North West Tonight.

"I'm confident that we made a substantial offer and it was knocked back.

"For various reasons, Denny became available through being fired from Castleford and once he'd been fired we got in touch and signed a contract."

It was again evident that the issue would rage long into the new 2017 Rugby League season.

TIGERS CONTINUE IN PERSUIT OF DAMAGES

Castleford Tigers went ahead with their claim that they should receive £500,000 in compensation after winger Denny Solomona left to join Sale Sharks in December. Solomona was alleged to have demanded his wages were doubled before his controversial rugby code switch.

Court papers seen by the BBC claimed that Sale had been agitating for Solomona to move since summer 2016, and that they acted with both the player and agent Andy Clarke. The papers also alleged that Sale knew he was under contract until November 2018.

Moreover, in an even more damning piece of evidence, the papers also claimed that Sale and the agent entered into a "cynical calculation" that they would be better off if the player breached his contract rather than negotiate a transfer fee.

The court papers included an email that Castleford said was sent by Sale's Director of Rugby Steve Diamond to the Tigers chief executive Steve Gill in which an offer of £50,000 compensation was made.

An earlier offer of £150,000 rising to £200,000 had been withdrawn.

In the email, it was claimed Diamond had written: "…legal advice has been sourced and we are confident that when he walks away he will be free to play Rugby Union.

"I… do not want to get the lawyers involved, it isn't our style and it will be a distraction as well as expensive to go through the courts for the next two years.

"The club are prepared to pay £50,000 immediately and you will release Denny from his contract at the end of September after your last match.

"Hopefully you will see the sense in a quick, quiet deal."

This arrogant approach of Diamond in insinuating that Sale and Rugby Union were somehow above Rugby League contracts and that Solomona could be bought with the meagre fee of £50,000 was a shocking revelation.

23rd February 2017

CAS ADJOURN COURT CASE

Castleford Tigers announced that they had adjourned their court case against Sale, which raised the prospect of an out-of-court settlement between the two clubs.

TIGERS HEAD TO COURT

Castleford returned to the courts in a bid to finally reach a settlement over the Denny Solomona saga.

The West Yorkshire club, at this time the Super League pace-setters which would be a position the Tigers would not relinquish, had been locked in negotiations since January in an attempt to find a resolution to the situation.

Castleford and Sale Sharks had broken off from court hearings to attempt to settle out of court, but the talks were unsuccessful and the case returned to Leeds' Mercantile Court.

16th June 2017

SETTLEMENT AGREED BETWEEN THE PARTIES

Finally, a settlement was reached between the Castleford Tigers and Sale Sharks over the issue that had raged for nigh-on eight months.

Castleford said they had accepted a settlement "in excess of £200,000" and ended their legal action against their former winger Denny Solomona, Sale Sharks and agent Andrew Clarke.

In addition to the compensation payment, Castleford say they will receive a substantial contribution, approximately £100,000, to their costs.

At the time of the transfer, Castleford Chief Executive Steve Gill said his club had started legal action "as a last resort", while Sale Director of Rugby Steve Diamond maintained that the Sharks had "acted legitimately".

Since switching to Rugby Union, Solomona had been capped by England and scored the winning try on his debut against Argentina on 10th June.

In response to the news that a settlement had been reached, RFL Chief Executive Nigel Wood: "Castleford have been resilient and professional throughout this entire process and the Rugby Football League and other member clubs have always fully supported them in defending a position that we believe is right and just."

The hero for Castleford in this drawn-out dispute, Chief Executive Steve Gill commented on the settlement: "This has been a difficult few months for the club.

"It would have been very easy to walk away and put all of this down to experience but Castleford Tigers is not a selling club anymore.

"We have demonstrated over the last three years that the club is ambitious. We want to maintain our existing squad and continue to improve."

This statement epitomised Gill and how he and the club had acted throughout the months: humble and respectful. Not one for the limelight, Gill had never spoken out of terms or commented on Sale's role in the whole issue, now he was just glad the saga was over and that Castleford could now move on.

What was brilliant to see was that Gill emphasised that the Tigers were no longer a selling club; a distinct contrast from the past. Gill had brought in this type of mindset when he became Chief Executive in 2013 and was the catalyst that had kickstarted Castleford's revival off the field. It was admirable to see him take on both Sale and the RFU and it was fantastic to see him, and the club as a whole, reap their just rewards for refusing to lie down.

PERFECT PRE-SEASON

LUKE GALE INKS NEW FIVE-YEAR DEAL UNTIL 2021

A Leeds Academy graduate, he found his first-team chances limited and moved to Doncaster where he established himself as one of the best players in the Championship and where he won the Young Championship Player of the Year in 2008. His performances attracted Super League interest, earning him a move to Harlequins RL for three years, before returning to West Yorkshire with Bradford Bulls in 2011

Gale joined the Tigers at the end of the 2014 season after the Bradford Bulls had been relegated and he has impressed ever since. During 2015, Gale instantly made his presence felt with a new-look Castleford team. Being at the heart of everything Castleford did well, Gale helped his side finish fifth in Super League. In doing so, Luke also earned the Albert Goldthorpe Medal for his performances, along with a call-up to the England team. Gale, along with teammate, Michael Shenton was also selected for the Super League Dream Team of 2015. Luke would go on to earn the Albert Goldthorpe Medal in 2016 and 2017, making him the first player to win it three times in a row.

He was already contracted for 2017, but there were strong rumours of a move away from the club. Gale said of his new deal: "I'm delighted to have signed my new deal with Castleford Tigers and it's great to be able to put all the rumours to bed. I love what Daryl and Steve are building here, it's a great club to be part of and I'm excited to see what the future holds for the club in the coming years. The fans are amazing and we've built a brilliant team here who are hungry for success and to bring silverware back to Castleford. I did have interest from elsewhere but I always wanted to stay here, and I'd like to see out the rest of my career here at Castleford Tigers."

Coach Daryl Powell had been mightily impressed with Gale's progress since joining the Tigers: "Luke Gale has been outstanding since he signed at Castleford Tigers and I expect him to improve every year he is with us.

"I fully expect him to become the next England half-back and look forward to him continuing to grow as a person and a player within our environment."

LARNE PATRICK SIGNS PERMANENT THREE-YEAR DEAL WITH THE TIGERS AFTER BEING ON LOAN

Larne Patrick, 27 at the time of signing, was initially on loan with Castleford from Huddersfield Giants, but would make the move permanent at the end of 2016 when his contract with the Giants ran out.

Welsh international Patrick signed for Huddersfield in 2009 and made over 100 appearances for the Giants, becoming a formidable asset that never took a backwards step.The 27-year-old spent the whole of the 2015 season on loan at Wigan and made 10 appearances for Huddersfield in 2016 before being told his contract would not be extended and thus, he signed on loan with the Tigers.

Patrick was delighted with the move: "I'm over the moon. It's a great club to be at. I've enjoyed the last five or six weeks and I'm really looking forward to the next three years here."

Powell was equally happy to add Patrick permanently to his squad: "We are delighted to confirm Larne will be with us for the next three years. "He is an experienced front rower whose line speed in defence, and ability to break the defensive line is outstanding. He has fitted in well while on loan and we feel he still has a lot of improvement in him."

GREG EDEN SIGNS A TWO-YEAR DEAL FROM BRISBANE BRONCOS

Eden began his Rugby League career with the Tigers, coming through Castleford's renowned academy setup. He made only four appearances for the club in 2011 before moving to Huddersfield Giants. He went on to play for Salford Red Devils and then Hull KR before trying his hand in the NRL with Brisbane Broncos at the end of the 2014 season. Whilst failing to make an appearance in his maiden year, he made seven appearances in 2016, but fell out of favour with coach Wayne Bennett, ironically the man who chose Eden as part of his England Elite Performance Squad for its second phase in the latter half of 2017.

Eden spoke of his joy at coming back to the club where it all started: "Coming back to the UK was a massive decision for me to make but there's no better team for me to return home to than Castleford, my hometown club and the team I grew up supporting. I'm really looking forward to the new challenge ahead."

Daryl Powell initially acquired Eden's services to fill the huge gap that the outgoing Luke Dorn would make at fullback: "I am delighted to say we have signed Greg Eden for the next two years. His athletic ability is exceptional which is key in order to play at full back in our team. I have been impressed with his development since he went to Australia and I am looking forward to seeing him achieve his rich potential with us over the coming years."

When Castleford signed Eden in June 2016, they did not realise the impact he would have in a position for which he was not originally signed. One cannot be sure whether, if Castleford had not signed Zak Hardaker, Greg would have played the same, crucial role he did on the wing in 2017, at fullback instead. But, fortunately for Castleford fans, he made the wing place his own.

RANGI CHASE JOINS CASTLEFORD UNTIL END OF SEASON WITH OPTION OF A FURTHER YEAR

The 30-year-old quit the game in May 2016 when he was released by Championship outfit Leigh. But he performed an about-turn to join the Tigers to the end of the season, with the club holding an option to extend the deal further.

Chase said of his move: "It's like coming back home for me, I love the people here. This move is purely about the badge and the way it made me feel when I played for it. I feel so blessed to be here and I thank God and everyone at this great club for giving me a second chance at Castleford Tigers."

Chase enjoyed most of his success during his five years at Castleford, where he scored 47 tries in 129 appearances from 2009-13 and was crowned Super League's Man of Steel in 2011. And Daryl Powell, who arrived too late in 2013 to halt Rangi's high-profile move to Salford was eager for Rangi to rekindle this kind of form.

Powell stated: "I am really pleased to be able to add to our squad at such a crucial stage in the season," Powell said. "Rangi is a high quality player who knows so much about Castleford Tigers and what it means to play for this club.

"It's a great opportunity for Rangi to make a big impact again in Super League and for us, it gives us great competition for places in such a key position as half-back. I look forward to welcoming Rangi to the club and seeing him pull on the famous shirt yet again."

RANGI CHASE SIGNS ONE-YEAR DEAL WITH THE OPTION OF A FURTHER YEAR

The 30-year-old former England international rejoined the Tigers as a free agent in July on a short-term contract until the end of the year and played in six of their last eight matches of the season. He did enough in those six matches to be rewarded with a new deal for 2017, with Castleford also having the option to extend it for a further year.

Chase was ecstatic to be given another chance by the club after they took a shock punt on him in July: "It's really good to come back. This year was about playing to see if the club wanted to keep me and I am over the moon.

"I've had some good times here and it's good to come back to a group that is capable of winning something in these next few years. We have a strong group of players and the club has turned around a lot from when I was last here."

Powell spoke of how much Rangi could impact the club positively on the field for 2017: "I am really pleased to retain Rangi for next season. He has fitted back into the club well and there is so much more to come from him.

"He has been out of the game for a while so his fitness levels need a pre-season but he has shown in his brief time back that there is still the talent and ability there.

"I am looking forward to seeing him grow into the way we play during pre-season and I am very confident he will be part of an awesome attacking threat for us next year and beyond."

MATT COOK PENS ONE-YEAR EXTENSION UNTIL 2018 WITH THE OPTION OF ANOTHER YEAR

Cook started his career with Bradford Bulls in 2003, where he was a member of the Bulls' World Club Challenge team that beat Wests Tigers in 2006. He made a brief loan move to the Tigers in 2008 where he appeared in three games. In 2010, Cook left Bradford for Hull KR, playing for two seasons in East Hull before heading south to the Broncos. Cook signed for Castleford at the end of 2014, following London's relegation from the Super League. He was already under contract for 2017.

Matt reiterated how much he was looking forward to the next few seasons: "It feels really good to get my new deal nailed down. It's been a tough year for the boys with all the injuries but to finish fifth was great for us. I've now got another two seasons to make sure I am around the club as I feel we'll be challenging for silverware and it's exciting times."

Powell also expressed how much he was excited by the potential role Matt could play with the Tigers for the next few years and, frighteningly, how much he could still improve: "Matt Cook has shown at the end of the season his potential as a player is still growing. I expect him to be a big part of an outstanding pack over the coming seasons and I am delighted he has agreed to extend his contract."

BRANDON DOUGLAS, 19, SIGNS NEW TWO-YEAR DEAL

Douglas joined the Tigers from Bradford Bulls' scholarship in 2013 and progressed through the Castleford Academy ranks. The new deal saw Douglas step up from the academy to the full-time first-team set up. 19 at the time, prop forward Douglas was drafted into the first-team after a string of injuries had taken their toll on Castleford's season and made his first-team debut against St Helens in early September in a heavy 40-16 defeat. Douglas however, impressed and earned the Tigers fans' Man of the Match vote.

Brandon was glad to be progressing to the first team and spoke of his desire to consolidate his future at the club: "I am looking forward to taking the step into a full-time environment with Castleford Tigers. I have spent the last three years in the Castleford academy system, which I have really enjoyed. With great support from the academy coaching and strength and conditioning team, I have developed as a player and I feel ready for a tough, honest pre-season! Castleford Tigers is a fantastic rugby club with amazing supporters. I was humbled by the support from the fans following my debut against St Helens and I'm looking forward to my future with Castleford Tigers."

Brandon showed in his one appearance last season that he is a player for the future who has no fear of any reputation as coach, Daryl Powell explained. "He was a stand-out performer in the under 19s competition last season and I have no doubt that a full pre-season under his belt will see him develop and grow into a tremendous front rower."

Brandon was sent on a season-long loan to Halifax RLFC for the 2017 season where he has continued to make significant strides, regularly impressing coach Richard Marshall.

JUNIOR MOORS PENS NEW TWO-YEAR CONTRACT UNTIL END OF 2019

Moors, a Samoan international, joined the Tigers on a three-year deal from Melbourne Storm ahead of the 2015 season. Previous to this, he had played over 50 NRL games for Wests Tigers, Penrith Panthers and Melbourne since making his debut in 2007. And after a relatively slow start to life in West Yorkshire, he swept the board at the club's presentation evening at the end of the 2016 season, picking up the Fans' Player of the Year, Players' Player of the Year and Player of the Year awards.

Junior stated how much he had settled at the club: "I'm really happy to have extended my deal with Cas. My family and I are really settled here and I love playing with these boys. 2017 will be a big season for us and I'm looking forward to the challenge ahead."

Powell also stressed just how much Junior had progressed in 2016 and how Moors could play the best rugby of his life at the club: "I'm delighted that Junior has agreed to extend his contract with the club. After a slow start in 2015, he had an enormous 2016, being one of the best forwards in Super League. His ball carry and skill as a forward gives us an extra dimension in our game. I have no doubt that he will continue to improve and we will see the very best of Junior Moors in the next few years."

CASTLEFORD SIGN LONDON YOUNGSTER TUOYO EGODO, 19, ON TWO-YEAR DEAL

Egodo had spent the previous three years with the Broncos' academy where he was sent on loan to League 1 side Hemel Stags in 2016. Impressing when present on the field, he scored one try in nine games.

Tuoyo was enthusiastic about making the step up to Super League level and told of how the move was too good to resist: "I'm extremely pleased to be signing for Castleford, a big club with a great fan base behind it! I feel like I have a lot to offer and can't wait to get stuck in with the lads. I'm looking forward to the move up north and I'm very excited to see what lies ahead over the coming years."

Powell was an admirer of the physical presence of the Londoner and was excited about Tuoyo's future at the club: "Tuoyo has come through the London system and looks a really exciting player for the future. He plays the game really physically and I'm really looking forward to seeing how he develops within our system. He is quick and strong with an ability to run straight over the top of people. He's just come out of under 19s Rugby League but he is certainly one to keep an eye on and I'm delighted he has agreed to sign at the Tigers."

18th October 2016

CASTLEFORD ADD DANIEL IGBINEDION, 22, FROM OXFORD RL ON TWO-YEAR DEAL

Daniel rose through the academy ranks at London Broncos before moving to Oxford. The promising prop or second-row played 21 times for the League 1 outfit during 2016, where he scooped the Most Improved Player award at the club's end of season awards. Daniel developed so well at Oxford in 2016 that he caught the eye of the Tigers coaching staff. From this interest, Daniel was invited by Tigers head coach Daryl Powell to spend a week in the full-time environment following positive reports by Oxford's head coach Tim Rumford, where he impressed enough to earn a contract.

Daniel was thrilled with the move to Castleford, whose fan base he'd admired: "I'm really thankful to Castleford Tigers for giving me the opportunity to further my rugby career. It's a fantastic opportunity for me and one that I will grab with both hands. I'm really looking forward to getting stuck into pre-season and getting to know my new teammates. Cas is a fantastic club with a great fan base and I can't wait to get started."

Powell was eager to see how Daniel could progress in a full-time environment: "Daniel played at Oxford last year and trained with us for a week during the season. He is exceptionally strong and determined to achieve his potential as a player. I'm keen to see how he develops within our system and I'm looking forward to working with him in his first full pre-season as a full-time player."

CASTLEFORD SIGN JESSE SENE-LEFAO ON TWO-YEAR DEAL FROM CRONULLA SHARKS

Sene-Lefao made his debut for Manly in 2013 and went on to play 38 games over three seasons with the NRL club. He then moved to Cronulla, making six appearances for the Sharks in 2016, but failed to be part of the team that ended the Sharks' Premiership drought.

Jesse brought international experience to the Tigers after making his Samoa debut in 2014 and has two caps with Toa Samoa. He had also played alongside current Castleford Tigers half-back, Ben Roberts in the 2014 Four Nations against England and is good friends with both Ben and fellow Samoan Junior Moors.

Jesse expressed how Castleford, with its passionate fan base, was the perfect fit for him to progress further as a player and person: "I'm really excited to be heading to the UK to join Castleford Tigers. I'm good friends with Ben Roberts and Junior Moors and they've both told me such positive stories about the club and how passionate the fans are."

"I'm ready now to take my game up to a new level and Castleford sounds perfect for me. I'm looking forward to playing for a club that plays such a big part in the community and my family and I are looking forward to the experience of moving overseas and getting to know the people of Castleford. We're taking a family holiday right now but I can't wait to make the move and knuckle down and show what I can do in pre-season training."

Powell admired how Jesse conducts himself on the field and spoke of how Jesse's time at Cronulla could benefit the Tigers: "I'm delighted that Jesse has agreed to join us. I watched him play two years ago for Manly and I was really impressed with his skill, energy, enthusiasm and determination as a player. This year he was in a great environment at the eventual winners of the NRL Cronulla Sharks and I'm sure he'll bring his great experience as a player to help us as a club achieve our goals."

GREG MINIKIN PENS NEW TWO-YEAR EXTENSION UNTIL 2019

Greg had signed on a two-year deal from York City Knights ahead of the 2016 season after coming through the ranks at the Knights. In 2016, he scored six tries in 16 appearances after forcing his way into an injury-laden Castleford side.

Greg was thrilled to have signed a new deal, seeing a rosy future at the club. "When my agent told me Cas wanted to extend, I was over the moon. I love it here at Cas and I'm really excited for next season.

"We have a bright future and we're aiming to win some silverware if not next year then in the near future. I'm really excited with what is going on at the club and we're really moving forward."

Powell rates Minikin highly and was happy with how he performed in his maiden season at the club, grasping the opportunities with both hands when called upon in 2016: "Greg Minikin became a real go-to last year.

"After we received so many injuries to the squad he quickly showed, he is at home in Super League. From his first game against Leeds all the way through the season, he challenged defences with his natural running style.

"I have no doubt he will be a big player in Castleford's future. I'm delighted he has extended his contract and look forward to seeing him improve further in the coming seasons."

DARYL POWELL SIGNS NEW DEAL UNTIL 2020

Since taking over from Ian Millward part way through the 2013 season, the former Leeds and Featherstone coach has worked wonders. In his three seasons with the club, Powell has taken Castleford to a Challenge Cup Final and Super League finishes of 4th, 5th and 5th.

Daryl was already part way through a five-year deal that he signed back in 2014 but both the club and Powell were more than happy to agree on a new contract after a few successful seasons. After retiring from a hugely successful career in 2001, Powell stepped into the breach as Leeds Rhinos' head coach. Just two years later and with the Rhinos sat top of Super League, Leeds parted ways with Powell and Tony Smith was brought in. Powell then spent time as Director of Rugby at Leeds before switching codes to coach Rugby Union side Leeds Tykes in 2005.

He returned to Rugby League in 2008 to coach Featherstone Rovers. Powell led Rovers to a Championship Grand Final win in 2011 and numerous top-place finishes before Castleford came calling.

Daryl spoke of his admiration for the club and how he wanted to be part of something special: "Although I signed a five-year contract a few years ago there was a get out clause at the end of next season which both the club and myself wanted to get rid of. I believe we are on the cusp of a very special period at Castleford and I want to be right at the heart of achieving something special with the group of players we have at the club at the moment."

"Right from the top of the club, starting with Ian Fulton working all the way through the management, the coaching staff and down to the players, we have special people working hard to achieve great times in Super League.

"We certainly have a lot of hard work in front of us, and although some of our mentality has to change, I believe we have everything in place to consistently challenge towards the top end of Super League and I'm delighted to extend my contract to hopefully play a major part in a special time in this great clubs future."

Chief Executive, Steve Gill, the man who kickstarted the Tigers' revival off the field and who brought Powell to the club, commended Powell on the way he transformed Castleford on the pitch and how he was key to the future of the Tigers: "On behalf of Ian Fulton and the Board of Directors I am pleased to announce that our Head Coach Daryl Powell has agreed a new four-year deal with the Castleford Tigers, Daryl has been very instrumental in the progress of our club in the past few years, and the reward of a new four-year contract reflects the trust and belief we have in him to bring silverware back to our great club."

PAUL McSHANE AGREES NEW DEAL UNTIL 2019

Paul began his career at Leeds Rhinos, graduating from its academy and making his debut in 2009. Since then, McShane has appeared in over 150 career games. Whilst half of these games came in a Rhinos jersey, McShane found opportunities at Leeds hard to come by during his stay in the first-team, resulting in two loan spells, first to Hull FC in 2010 and then to Widnes Vikings in 2012.

In 2014, the hooker moved to Wakefield, eager for first-team action. He became one of their most consistent performers. Then, in a swap deal that saw Scott Moore move to the Wildcats, McShane moved to Castleford just before the transfer deadline in 2015.

In 2016, McShane made his mark on the Castleford team, being an integral cog in the Tigers' wheel, playing in 32 games and scoring seven tries. Paul also demonstrated his ability to play half-back after injuries had forced Powell to make a host of changes and McShane did not disappoint.

Upon signing the extension, Paul was undoubtedly cheerful and articulated how much the club and town means to him and his family: "It's a big thing for my family to be re-signing with the Tigers. My wife loves it at this club and that makes it a lot easier for me. From day one coming in midway through last year, I knew it was a club that was for me. The way that people are around here is great."

"You come in every day with a group of good people and all they want to do is make you better and that's throughout the coaches, players and everyone else at the club," McShane added. "Then you come to game day and you've got the fans. When you come to training sometimes at 7 or 8 in the morning you're guaranteed to see a couple of Cas shirts walking round the streets and to have fans like that who back you as a team that much, it's just something I want to be a part of."

Powell was over the moon to see Paul extend his contract and conveyed how Paul should be striving for international recognition whilst at the Tigers: "Paul McShane has always been a very good player but I thought we started to see how good he can really be towards the middle and back end of last season. He is a natural ball player who understands the game very well. I have no doubt he is going to improve, and although he has a host of competition at international level, I think he is one of the most natural hookers in Rugby League and should strive to attain that level. I look forward to working with him during his extended contract and I'm delighted he wants to stay at the Tigers"

BEN CROOKS JOINS LEIGH ON SEASON-LONG LOAN

Centre Ben Crooks came through the ranks at Hull FC, making his debut in 2012. His breakthrough season with Hull came in 2013 when he was named in the Super League Dream Team after scoring 20 tries in 22 games in a prolific partnership with winger Tom Lineham. 2014 failed to see him rekindle the same form and he left the Airlie Birds for NRL club Parramatta Eels. He returned to England at the end of 2015, heading to Castleford on a three-year contract. He made 28 appearances for the Tigers in 2016 and scored six tries.

Castleford however, allowed the centre to join Leigh on a season-long loan for 2017. The move freed up both a squad place and room in the Tigers' salary cap for Hardaker, who was announced as a Castleford player a day later.

Powell spoke of the necessity for Crooks to get game time, pointing to the fact that he would be behind Shenton, Webster and Minikin in the pecking order: "Ben had a really solid first season with us last year and played a number of games in the first-team.

"However, with the return to fitness of Michael Shenton and the emergence of Greg Minikin as a quality centre, I thought it was really important that Ben played consistent Rugby League game time.

"This loan move gives him a great opportunity to do that at Leigh next season. I'm confident that Ben will continue to improve throughout the next Super League season and I wish him all the best in 2017 at Leigh Centurions."

ZAK HARDAKER JOINS TIGERS ON SEASON-LONG LOAN WITH A VIEW TO A PERMANENT DEAL

Zak Hardaker burst onto the scene as a Featherstone Rovers player, then coached by Daryl Powell in 2010, scoring 27 tries in 19 appearances and being named Championship Young Player of the Year. In October 2010, Zak moved to Leeds Rhinos for £60,000 where he won multiple Super League titles and two Challenge Cups, scoring 67 tries in 155 appearances in the process. Hardaker was named Man of Steel in 2015 after being an influential figure in the Rhinos' treble-winning campaign. Under a cloud of personal problems however, Zak spent the latter half of the 2016 season on loan at NRL club Penrith Panthers, playing 11 games and scoring one try.

The deal meant that Zak would remain at Castleford for the full season with no recall provision and was free to play against Leeds when the two sides met. Castleford also secured the option to complete a full transfer from November 2017 for an undisclosed transfer fee already agreed by both clubs. The permanent transfer was completed in June instead.

The Tigers beat off stiff competition from Huddersfield and Salford to conclude the high-profile deal, with Zak adamant that the time was right for the move: "I'm in a really good place, so that's why I can't wait to get started."

On the move, Powell stressed how much of a good player Zak was and drew on his own experience of working with him to underline how Zak could improve the Tigers. Powell also strongly believed that the move could bring Zak back into the England fold: "I am delighted that Zak has decided to sign for the Tigers. Two years ago he was the Man of Steel and there is no doubt he is an outstanding Rugby League player. His flexibility in playing a number of positions in the backline will clearly enhance what is already a very talented squad and add quality competition. I have worked with Zak in the past and look forward to seeing him enhance his own reputation as a Rugby League player and get back into the England team as a Castleford Tigers player."

TIGERS THRASH YOUTHFUL HULL SIDE

Greg Eden registered an impressive hat-trick in his first came back for the Tigers since his departure in 2011. Mike McMeeken was the first to score when Rangi Chase, given the No.6 jersey by Powell, put him over. By the halfway point in the first-half, Castleford were up 10-0 after Zak Hardaker, playing for his new club for the first time since his high-profile loan from big-city rivals Leeds Rhinos, added to the scores. Greg Minikin would get his first just minutes later and then add a second just before half-time after Eden had grabbed his first in-between Minikin's efforts. With a 24-0 lead, the Tigers were seemingly out of sight by the time the second forty got underway. The one-way traffic continued after the break when Eden scooped up a kick to dance past three would-be defenders, hand off a fourth and scorch away for the try of the day. Unbeknown to the Tigers' fans on Boxing Day, this demonstration of electrifying pace and classy skill from the winger would be a regular, thrilling occurrence throughout 2017. Eden would complete his hat-trick on the hour mark to make it 32-0. 32 became 42 soon after as Tuoyo Egodo and Luke Million were the grateful recipients of wonderful attacking play, the type with which the Tigers would light up Super League. Powell rang the changes with the likes of under 19 stars, Declan Sheehan and Luis Johnson, getting game time and the lack of experience in the final 20 minutes showed for the Tigers as the visitors crossed twice through Callum Lancaster and Jez Litten. It was a good runout for the Tigers, but up against a Hull side which featured very few regulars, it did not provide Powell with the sort of game he would have liked in order to prepare for the season ahead.

WHAT THE FANS SAID

@JonnyG88: "Denny Who?!"

@James27LUFC: "Cas Tigers smashed Hull and Leeds battered Preston! Great Boxing Day for me!"

A TALE OF TWO HALVES AS THE WILDCATS PIP THE TIGERS

After a comfortable win over a young Hull FC team on Boxing Day, the Tigers were to travel to their 'nearest and dearest', Wakefield Trinity. The first-half belonged purely to the visitors, who fielding a strong line-up which included all three half-backs, were simply too strong.

The Tigers opened their account in the fourth minute as Ben Roberts put in a delightful grubber kick on which his half-back partner, Luke Gale could pounce. Castleford's next try came in the resulting set from a Gale 40/20, a common occurrence in 2017, as neat hands by Gale and Greg Eden, playing at full-back in the absence of Zak Hardaker, fed Minikin in the corner. Gale converted both and was on target again after Paul McShane, one of Castleford's finest performers throughout the year, burrowed over from dummy half after Tuoyo Egodo was brought down just shy of the line.

The Tigers continued to knock on the Trinity door and soon, the door collapsed as Eden magnificently caught a low Gale pass to finish superbly. Gale maintained his perfect kicking rate with yet another conversion to make it 24-0 just before half-time. The hosts did however finally make headway before the hooter as Reece Lyne reached out to score after Eden had had the ball stolen as he was returning a kick. With the conversion unsuccessful, the Tigers were up 24-4 at half-time. Even when the second forty resumed, so did Castleford's scoring spree as youngster Luke Million sold an outrageous dummy to scoot over from dummy half after Wakefield winger Tom Johnstone had dropped the ball from the restart. The Trinity star would sadly miss most of the season with a ruptured anterior cruciate ligament suffered in May. Eden's goal, deputising for Gale who had left the field, made it 30-4.

As Powell rang the changes with eight academy players coming on, Trinity slowly forced their way back into contention. First, Sam Williams went over and converted his own score on 47 minutes. Then centre Bill Tupou found the line after Ben Jones-Bishop had been hauled down by Rangi Chase following a break. Minutes later, Wakefield teenager James Batchelor broke through a youthful Tigers defence to set up the position for Joe Arundel to score off a neat kick by Trinity half-back Jacob Miller. None of these tries were converted by Williams though, and Trinity were still eight behind as the scores read 22-30.

By now, the momentum was well and truly with the home side and Johnstone was the next to profit as he somehow got the ball down in the corner despite the attention of the Castleford defence. And minutes before the final hooter, the hosts secured a stunning comeback when Anthony Walker powered over from close range. With Williams' second conversion of the day, Trinity went into the lead for the first time, 32-30.

Wakefield held on to continue their good pre-season form. For the Tigers, the match showed how well Powell's team could play when many of the first-teamers were on the field, but it also gave vital experience to youngsters such as Tom Holmes, who would play a key part in the Tigers' memorable year. For Powell, the end result was of no concern; that first-half had demonstrated that something special was definitely in the offing. Over the course of the season, this would prove correct.

WHAT THE FANS SAID

@tigerbarry13: "Trinity were never in the game til Cas took Gale,Roberts,Lynch, McShane, Milner off on 40minutes then Webster, Eden"

@RobbieRLrussel: "credit cas for leaving young blokes on-- they will learn heaps from that . It would have been easy to throw the big guns back out"

BRANDON WESTERMAN RELEASED BY THE TIGERS

Westerman, who signed a new contract with Castleford in 2016, requested a release from his contract, a wish that the club granted. Despite impressing in the Tigers' under 19s setup, Brandon failed to break into the first-team squad and made several appearances for York City Knights in the latter half of the 2016 season.

On his release, Castleford chief executive Steve Gill remarked that the club wanted to honour his intentions: "Brandon requested a release from his contract last weekend, and after a short discussion as a club, it was agreed that it would be the right thing to allow him to move on."

25th January 2017

TIGERS SIGN JAKE TRUEMAN FROM BRADFORD BULLS

Jake, just 17 years of age at the time, had progressed through the Bulls academy and made his first-team debut in May 2016 in a 54-8 drubbing of Swinton. Trueman had been highly rated by his previous coaches and Powell admitted that he was looking forward to seeing him develop within the Tigers environment.

Speaking while on the club's pre-season camp, Powell said: "Jake is a young player who became available after the difficulties that Bradford faced in the recent past. We are delighted to acquire the services of a talented young half-back who has a big future in the game."

Powell added: "He has already played first-team football at Bradford and is a talented all-round half-back. We now have some of the best young half-backs in the country in our system to learn from the quality that we have in our first-team. This means our future is very rosy in the decision-making department."

On his move, Jake remarked: "I wanted to join Castleford because of the coaching staff on board, I think they can develop and improve me as a player. The club just feels like the right fit for me. I am really looking forward to meeting my new teammates and training under these coaches and developing my skills as a half-back."

BATLEY BLITZ YOUNG TIGERS

On a bitterly cold Friday night, the Tigers, whose only players that would go on to appear for the first team in 2017 were Kieran Gill, Tom Holmes, Will Maher, Tuoyo Egodo and Jake Trueman, were simply no match for a full-strength Bulldogs side. The visitors could not have made a worse start as the Tigers knocked on from the kick-off, and from the resulting set, second-rower James Harrison forced his way over and would do so again a few minutes later following a great Dominic Brambani break.

By the ninth minute, the hosts had their third try as fullback Dave Scott went through some soft defending to touch down beside the posts. The onslaught continued as a neat Brambani kick was hacked on by Sam Smeaton with his winger Wayne Reittie pouncing on the loose ball. With Pat Walker landing two out of four conversions, the Bulldogs led 20-0 inside 15 minutes. By now, the young Tigers were desperate and needed to hold out to have any chance at all of recovering what seemed like an impossible situation.

To their credit, the visitors clawed their way back into proceedings. First, Kieran Gill took a smart Holmes offload, and moments before the break, a superb cut-out pass by Conor Fitzsimmons sent Declan Sheehan in at the corner. Two conversions by Jake Sweeting, the second a magnificent touchline effort in horrendous conditions, brought the Tigers back within eight points of the Bulldogs as the half-time siren went. Batley, however, were in no mood to allow their visitors to reduce the deficit further and instead, they pulled further ahead four minutes after the restart as Alex Rowe, a Castleford academy product, scooped up Alistair Leak's offload to dot down underneath the posts with Brambani converting.

Although the Tigers continued to have their moments, it was the home side who extended their lead further with the try of the game as half-backs Cain Southernwood and Brambani linked up to send Scott through a gaping hole in the Tigers' defence for his second. And just seven minutes before full-time, Batley completed the scoring when substitute James Davey fed an onrushing Brad Hill. Southernwood took over the kicking duties and succeeded with his first attempt.

It was a satisfactory victory for Matt Diskin's men, who had now won three pre-season friendlies out of three, but Powell would have been pleased with how some of his young chargers showed their mettle in difficult conditions, not least the performance of Tom Holmes who demonstrated he was ready for Super League. He would go on to partake in some crucial cameos for the Tigers during 2017.

WHAT THE FANS SAID

@PhilDransfield: "not bad from Cas against a good tough Batley side, hope the game was played in the right manner"

TIGERS TOPPLE SAINTS TO END HOODOO

The Totally Wicked Stadium as the Saints' stadium is now called, witnessed a totally dominant performance from the Tigers in what was their first victory at St Helens since 1990. Just two minutes into the game, the visitors recorded their first points as Rangi Chase, who would sadly leave the Tigers midway through the season after successive disciplinary issues, showed great acceleration and trickery to work his way through the Saints defence after the home side had failed to deal with a Luke Gale bomb. The latter converted to make it 6-0.

It would take another 23 minutes for the next score as Zak Hardaker dummied and sauntered through a massive gap for a Luke Dorn-esque effort. Gale's conversion hit the posts, but the Tigers would go into the break 10-0 up. The visitors continued their ascendancy after the restart as a Chase kick forced a goal-line drop-out. From the repeat set, Gale sent Jesse Sene-Lefao over for his first try in Castleford colours. How Jesse asserted himself in this game and the fashion in which he scored and celebrated this try demonstrated just how much of an impact he would have at the club in 2017. A real character on and off the field, Jesse would go on to embody the Castleford culture that Powell and everyone else at the club had been building.

The towering figure of Grant Millington would be the next over the whitewash as he held off three defenders to touch down. Gale converted both tries and the Tigers' scoring ended there. Saints would finally get on the board, but only in lucky circumstances. A 40/20 attempt by the hosts' half-back Danny Richardson was kept spectacularly in play by Greg

Eden, but sadly for Eden, the nearest player to the ball was Adam Swift who gratefully gobbled up possession to register Saints' first points of the afternoon. With Percival converting, the Tigers led 22-6 and this is how the match would finish.

Coach Daryl Powell had emphasised in pre-season that his side had been focusing on tightening up their defence which had been so leaky in the past. It certainly showed, as the Tigers limited St Helens' go-forward and forced them to only attempt to attack from deep, and even more impressive, Saints' only try came on the back of a Tigers mistake. This was a victory that well and truly epitomised the Tigers in 2017: commanding, determined and exciting.

WHAT THE FANS SAID

@Fatboy_Rob: "10 out of 10 performance for Cas against a strong Saints team. 1st time I've ever seen Cas win over here #COYF"

@Castigers_JT: "Great defence from the lads today played well Cas 22 Saints 6 #COYF"

@nickpreston123: "Friendly or not, just seen Cas win away at saints for the first time #COYF"

@LewisThomp_93: "Defence been immense!"

FINE
FEBRUARY

#1 - Zak Hardaker

Date of Birth: 17/10/1991
Height: 189cm (6 ft 2)
Weight: 92kg (14.5 stone)
Country: England
Position: Full-back
Previous Clubs: Featherstone Rovers, Leeds Rhinos, Penrith Panthers (loan)
National Honours: 3 caps for England Knights, 5 caps for England

Super League Stats Throughout:

Appearances: 28	**Avg. Gain:** 8.29
Tries: 12	**Tackles:** 220
Try Assists: 18	**Clean Breaks:** 16
Metres: 3257	**Offloads:** 25

Zak was brought to the Tigers on a season-long loan from big city rivals Leeds Rhinos, to replace Luke Dorn. Zak was a more defensively minded full-back but in 2017, he emerged as a confident attacking player whose judgement and execution played a significant role in the success of the potent left-side attack for the Tigers.

Superb length-of-the-field efforts against his former club at Headingley and against Catalans in Perpignan endeared him to the Tigers fans who had cast the Featherstone man as their number one enemy when he played for Leeds. His apparent new level-headedness and reliability, as well as the emphatic return to his 2015 form which earned him the prestigious Man of Steel, explains why he won both Player of the Year and the highly-coveted Players' Player of the Year at the Tigers' awards ceremony in September as well as a place in the Super League 2017 Dream Team and the Man of Steel shortlist where he finished second to teammate Luke Gale by 32 votes.

Zak also appeared to transform as a person in 2017, regularly participating in the Tigers' community work and having photos with and chatting with fans at local events. In June 2017, Zak signed a four-and-a-half year deal at the Tigers which would have seen him play at the club until 2021. A £150,000 fee was paid, largely from the Denny Solomona court case. This fee was yet another sign of how far the Tigers had come since their financial troubles a few years ago.

Yet, in Grand Final week, all of Zak's self-confessed development off the field came to nothing as he was dropped for a 'breach of club rules'. It was later revealed that he had failed a drugs test, taken following Castleford's victory against Leeds in mid-September. After seemingly reigniting his career with the Tigers and with the club forking out massive money for Zak, the way in which he let his teammates down before the most important match in Castleford's history was a bitter pill to swallow. His absence was a key factor in the Grand Final disappointment.

 **@AaronBower – 17th August 2017:** "Zak Hardaker at his absolute best right there. That's why so many people are convinced he's England's No.1 for the World Cup. Devastating."

CASTLEFORD PUT THEIR CONFIDENT WORDS INTO ACTION

The talking up of Castleford's chances for the upcoming season was over. It was time to let their play on the field do the talking. Their first opponents were the newly-promoted Leigh Centurions, who received a baptism of fire in their first fixture back in the top flight. After withstanding heavy pressure from the visitors for the opening 15 minutes, Castleford underlined why so many pundits predicted them for the top. In the 19th minute, substitute Grant Millington displayed his ball-handling skills, feeding his half-back Luke Gale with a wonderful offload for the first try of the night.

Then, just five minutes later, Millington was at it again as he timed his pass to new recruit Jesse Sene-Lefao to perfection. Winger Greg Minikin was then the joyful recipient of, what would become customary for the Tigers, free-flowing Rugby League as he went over for two tries in the last ten minutes of the half, the second of which was put on a plate for him after a typically muscular run from the evergreen Jake Webster. With Luke Gale converting all four tries, as well as adding a penalty near half-time, the hosts went into the break with a 26-0 lead.

If the Tigers weren't out of sight by half-time, they soon were after it; with barely two minutes on the clock, prop Junior Moors barged his way over from short range. Leigh's Ryan Hampshire, who spent 2016 on loan at the Tigers, then recorded the Centurions' first points back in Super League. Yet, the visitors could not stem the tide and Hampshire went from hero to zero in the 57th minute, fumbling Gale's high kick who then dribbled the ball to touch down after having something of a battle with Greg Eden. Eden soon got his try though as skipper Michael Shenton fed him with a neat pass four minutes later. Gale converted both and ended the night with eight from eight.

With the game dead and buried, Leigh did add some respectability to the scoreline as Matty Dawson and Danny Tickle both scored converted tries. The night, however, belonged to the Tigers. Raved about by the media, the Tigers certainly did not disappoint in what seemed a potentially tough fixture on paper.

Whilst leaking 16 points was something of a disappointment, 10 of these did come when the game was effectively over. Moreover, the sensational attacking play the Tigers displayed was a pure joy to watch and set the tone for the breath-taking style of play that would become a customary feature whenever Castleford took to the field.

WHAT THE FANS SAID

@JakeMaw: "I feared a loss tonight, oh how wrong was I?! #Coyf #SweetCaroline."

@charlotteroseg_: "Great result and still loads to work on. Yeahhhh the boyss."

@BarbaraHirst55: "Nice little opening game for the Tigers. Played some nice rugby on a heavy pitch. Negatives were discipline & cue on rack for 10mins. #amhappy."

@PhilDransfield: "Got to be happy with avoiding that banana skin #DifferentLeague #RugbyLeague #SLCasLei #COYF."

@LMacca1: "Job done lots to improve on but some good team spirit and plenty of positives looking forward to the journey #castigers."

KEVIN LARROYER SIGNS ONE-YEAR DEAL WITH AN OPTION OF A FURTHER TWO YEARS

Kevin began his career at Toulouse where he was snapped up by Catalans Dragons ahead of the 2012 season after impressing in his first two years with the club. He left the Dragons on loan to Hull KR ahead of the 2014 season. He excelled in Humberside making 22 appearances for the Robins and scoring seven tries. Kevin's loan deal was extended by the club for another year for the upcoming 2015 season. Larroyer was part of the Hull KR Challenge Cup final team in 2015. Then, in September 2015, the French international committed his future to Hull Kingston Rovers by signing a 3-year deal until the end of 2018. Kevin has also made 14 appearances for France during his career.

Unfortunately, Kevin was left without a club following Hull KR's relegation from Super League in the Million Pound Game at the end of 2016 and did spend time training with Hull FC. The Black and Whites, however, made it clear that they had no space on their salary cap for Larroyer, but they did give him the option to train with them to maintain his fitness levels whilst searching for a new club.

Upon signing Larroyer, the Tigers immediately loaned him to the Bradford Bulls for much-needed game time with Castleford having the option to recall him at 24 hours' notice after he had spent at least 28 days with Bradford.

Kevin was understandably thrilled to be thrown a lifeline by Castleford: "I'm absolutely delighted to sign for Castleford. To be part of this squad and this club is an honour. I've played at the Jungle a few times against Castleford and I've always thought the fans and the atmosphere were amazing. I'm looking forward to embracing this challenge and giving my best to Castleford Tigers."

Powell was enthusiastic about Kevin bringing serious competition for places in the forwards: "Kevin will add depth to our squad while we still have Larne Patrick and Oliver Holmes out injured. Kevin is a player who is proven at Super League level and did a really good job for Hull KR. He can play in the back row and in the middle unit as well which gives us some real depth and competition for places, which will be really valuable as we move into the Easter period,"

Powell added: "He is a French player who came over here to really challenge himself, and who played consistently for Hull HR. He runs good lines and he's a pretty tough and durable guy whom I'm looking forward to working with."

ALEX FOSTER JOINS ON A TRIAL WITH A VIEW TO A PERMANENT TWO-YEAR DEAL

Alex came through the Leeds Rhinos Academy and made his Super League debut for the Rhinos in 2013, going on to make eight more appearances that season. Despite signing a three-year contract at the end of 2013, he spent all of 2014 on loan at London Broncos and all of 2015 on loan at Featherstone Rovers. In 2016, he moved back to Londo, this time permanently, on a two-year deal and went on to make 20 appearances, scoring 11 tries in the process. But, ahead of the 2017 season, he relocated north once more to Bradford Bulls after signing a two-year contract. Yet, Alex became a free agent once the Bulls went into liquidation. With seemingly nowhere in the rugby world to go and plagued by injury, Foster thought long and hard about retiring and pursuing other career avenues.

Castleford however offered Alex a lifeline. The Tigers brought Alex in on an initial trial basis with the view of signing a two-year contract once he recovered from an operation that kept him out of action for four weeks.

Alex was undoubtedly overjoyed by the chance given to him by the Tigers: "I'm really excited about the opportunity. It was a no-brainer when I found out there was some interest. Castleford is a great club with a proud history. They have gone from strength to strength in the last few years."

Upon the announcement of the trial, Powell revealed his long-term admiration of Foster: "Alex is a player I have always been impressed with since his time at London when he played against us when London were last in Super League.

"With Larne Patrick and Oliver Holmes both still injured, I think we are looking a little bit skinny moving forward, especially towards the Easter period and so I thought it was a great opportunity to get Alex in."

As seen later, Alex did enough to impress in his trial period to secure himself a deal with the club and, in turn, secure his once uncertain future.

GADWIN SPRINGER SIGNS NEW TWO-YEAR DEAL UNTIL 2019

Born in French Guiana, Gadwin became the first player from South America to play in Super League with his Catalans bow. Known for his immense power at such a young age, Springer joined Catalans in 2012 from Toulouse after being highlighted as a star in the French media.

The junior French international made his debut for the Dragons in 2014 against St Helens. Gadwin had only made three substitute appearances for Catalans in 2015 before Castleford snapped him up midway through that season.

Before signing this deal, Gadwin had made 31 appearances for the Tigers and had developed into a real crowd favourite with his strong and aggressive running.

Gadwin was delighted to extend his contract at his 'home from home': "I feel very happy to be staying at Castleford for two more years. Since I have come here, I have improved a lot and I think of Cas as my second home now,"

"I think it is great that the fans chant for me and I appreciate how they support the team. I just love playing at The Jungle! We have a great side and I hope we can win something soon. I think that if we go through the season with no injuries we can achieve something great here at the Tigers."

Powell saw a big future for the monster prop at the club and praised his work ethic: "Gadwin has worked exceptionally hard since he has been at the club to develop all aspects of his game. He is a big physical specimen whose ball carries are a real threat to the opposition's defence. I have no doubt he will continue to improve and develop into an all-round outstanding front rower of the future and I'm delighted that he has agreed to extend his contract at the club."

#2 - Greg Minikin

Date of Birth: 29/03/1995
Height: 181cm (5 ft 9)
Weight: 88kg (13.8 stone)
Country: England
Position: Centre/Wing
Previous Clubs: York City Knights,
Batley Bulldogs (loan)

Appearances: 27	**Avg. Gain:** 8.44
Tries: 19	**Tackles:** 174
Try Assists: 6	**Clean Breaks:** 24
Metres: 2668	**Offloads:** 18

After bursting onto the scene quite dramatically midway through the 2016 season, Greg made the wing spot his own in 2017, despite his preferred position being centre. With remarkable strength for his size, Minikin developed so quickly under Powell's tutelage that there had been calls for him to be considered for an England spot ahead of the World Cup. Before the season started, Cas fans were concerned that Solomona's departure had not been covered. At the club's shirt launch, however, it was clear that Powell felt Minikin could make the step up as Greg was given the number 2 shirt. And boy was Powell correct. 2017 saw Greg mature faster than anyone had predicted, his early-season moustache also played a key role in his 'coming-of-age!', as he recorded a superb 15 tries in just the opening 18 games.

Whilst Castleford's left-side attack stole the show, Greg was a deadly finisher on the Tigers' right and ended the season as the fifth highest Super League scorer with 19 (with three Challenge Cup tries, he ended the season with a 22-try haul). Greg also demonstrated a type of power that belied his stature and size. His most impressive moment in a Castleford shirt in 2017 had to be his try in Castleford's first defeat, at the hands of Salford in March. Greg was given the ball by his centre Jake Webster 30 metres out from the Red Devils' line with three defenders around him. Greg, unfazed, rampaged to the try-line, carrying all three defenders with him, even the juggernaut that is Justin Carney. Despite being injured in the process of scoring and feared to be out for a while, Greg missed only two games, making his return in Castleford's victory away at Wigan in April.

Not only was his attack purring, but he helped valiantly in defence, often against opponents far bigger than him, as well as aiding his forwards by taking strong carries when the Tigers were coming out of their own half. The step up he made from his time at York was brilliant to see in 2017 and, although he is far from the finished product, the 2017 season really was a breakthrough year for Greg. It is evident that Greg has a bright future in the game and 2018 promises to showcase his potential even further.

@tombryan93 – 23rd June 2017: "Wow! To catch and step like that from @greg_minikin is something else! #someplayer #englandcentre."

@grahamsmithctsc – 23rd June 2017: "Does anyone know when @greg_minikin is letting Kallum Watkins out of his pocket? @CTRLFC #seveninarow #topoftheleague."

THE TIGERS HUNT DOWN THE WOLVES

An even tougher fixture on paper beckoned for Castleford as they faced Warrington, two weeks after their home battering of Leigh. The Tigers' two-week break was down to the Wolves partaking in the World Club Series, where they had emphatically brushed aside the Brisbane Broncos.

Still on a high from that ground-breaking victory, the Wolves were the quickest out of the blocks; Ryan Atkins was first denied a try for a forward pass and then Daryl Clark was held up over the line. But the hosts did cross in the sixth minute when Andre Savelio, who was a prominent figure for the Tigers whilst on loan at the end of the 2016 season, scooped up a loose ball to force his way over after Rhys Evans had palmed back a towering Kevin Brown kick.

Castleford were struggling with Warrington's intensity as the fortnight break seemed to have done the Tigers no favours, yet a devastating spell beginning midway through the first-half saw the visitors rack up four tries in eight minutes. First, Jesse Sene-Lefao went on a powerful diagonal run to canter past the hapless Wolves defence, then Mike McMeeken went on a similarly impressive run from a Rangi Chase pass around halfway to send Zak Hardaker away for a stunning try. A blistering response became even more remarkable when Gale and Hardaker got Eden over in a right-to-left move that would become a common occurrence throughout 2017, although Gale failed to convert for the first time. The onslaught was completed when, from the resulting Wire kick-off, Hardaker, just ten metres from his own line, went on a mazy run picking holes in the hosts' tired defence before feeding the supporting Gale for a scintillating score that had the Tigers fans and the Sky Sports commentary team in raptures.

The Wolves finally managed to stem the tide and did eventually hit back themselves three minutes from the break when Lineham burrowed his way over from close range to reduce the deficit to 12 points at half-time. That deficit was cut even further midway through the second-half when Brown's long pass saw Lineham claim his second try of the night with a spectacular dive in at the corner. Patton landed a superb touchline conversion to leave the home side just six points behind.

The Tigers, now the team under pressure, claimed the momentum back once again with a superb individual effort by Greg Minikin after Adam Milner had created an opening following a determined run from his own half. Savelio was to claim his second seven minutes later, taking advantage of soft defending to set up a tense finale. But the Tigers

had the last word as Eden recorded his second of the night just five minutes from the end after another smart move down the Tigers' left.

A combination of finesse and resolve had seen the Tigers keep the Wolves at bay and then overwhelm them with skill and panache that Super League had been missing for too long. A much-talked-about victory that validated the decision to bring Hardaker to the club, the Tigers had inflicted a hard-fought and well-deserved defeat on 2016's league leaders.

WHAT THE FANS SAID

@siroe31: "Dare to dream? @CTRLFC great performance tonight by the boys. Some awesome tries and playing for each other and the shirt."

@Stulake65: "This Castleford side are something special"… Maybe we are. We just went toe to toe with a nailed on contender and won."

@nogis: "What an amazing performance @CTRLFC."

@ianhenshaw1983: "Great performance by Cas, iron out soft tries and we're gonna be even better. Great win."

@becky_allatt: "Great result for the @CTRLFC tonight!! Shame I couldn't make it over…well played lads #Tigers4Life."

MEMORABLE MARCH

#3 - Jake Webster

Date of Birth: 29/10/1983
Height: 181cm (5 ft 9)
Weight: 101kg (15.9 stone)
Country: New Zealand/Britain
Position: Centre
Previous Clubs: Melbourne Storm, Gold Coast Titans, Hull Kingston Rovers
National Honours: 8 Caps for New Zealand

Appearances: 26	**Avg. Gain:** 7.73
Tries: 14	**Tackles:** 410
Try Assists: 14	**Clean Breaks:** 15
Metres: 2126	**Offloads:** 23

Well, what can a Castleford fan say about Jake Webster? He is like a fine wine: he gets better with age. A firm fans' favourite, he finishes every match knowing full well he has put his body and his opponents through the ringer and yet is one of the most pleasant players off the field to ever wear the Tigers shirt. Jake always has time for the fans and one can guarantee that he is the last to exit the field after taking pictures and shaking hands with the Castleford fans.

In 2017, Jake showed no signs of weakness on the field and in games where he was absent, the gap he left was often gaping. Minikin's try-scoring exploits owed a great deal to Webster's centre-play, attracting defenders and creating the space for Greg to finish. Jake's bruising style and formidable running was on display more so than ever in 2017, whilst his superb defensive game almost always stopped his opponents firmly in their tracks. The 'Hulk-ish' way he conducts himself on the field and the respect he commands deep within the club, was a key factor in him receiving the Directors' Player of the Year at the Tigers' awards ceremony in September.

When Jake came to Castleford in 2013 on a three-year deal, many believed the contract would take him to retirement following a series of devastating injuries. But after more severe injuries, not least the six-month lay-off with his knee back in 2013, Jake overcame these problems to propel himself to being one of the first names on the teamsheet. When Jake finally retires, although this date is still a mystery as he appears to be rolling back the years in emphatic fashion, he will go down in history as being a Castleford great. And irrespective of his wounds, his gleaming smile is always there to see after the final hooter when he approaches the fans.

When he does stop playing, all Castleford fans would love to see Jake take on some sort of coaching role within the club. An adopted Tiger, Castleford is Jake's home.

 **@M_Shaw1 – 17th August 2017:** "Jake Webster a hero around these parts anyway. He's ensured tonight he'll forever be remembered though. Brilliant display."

'CLASSY CAS' DESTROY THE RHINOS WITH EASE

Castleford's two previous victories against Leigh and Warrington were impressive, but this thrashing of their local rivals was done in such an emphatic fashion, it made the whole Rugby League fraternity sit up and take note. Leeds simply had no answer to the exuberant, almost theatrical, style of play exhibited by the Tigers. The 'Classy Cas' brand, rejuvenated in recent years, was displayed throughout, not least when Junior Moors broke in midfield after fending off three would-be tacklers in the 16th minute. Luke Gale was in support, as all good halves should be, and was fed with a one-handed offload. Sidestepping his way over the halfway line, Gale produced an inch-perfect kick to the corner for Greg Minikin to collect superbly and dot down over the whitewash. This was just one of three first-half tries for Greg Minikin and these scores, along with a brace from Greg Eden, following great link-up play from Gale and Zak Hardaker, and one from Mike McMeeken meant the Tigers were 30-0 up at the break.

The Tigers never looked back after the half-time whistle as Hardaker, playing against the Rhinos for the first time since his clouded future with the club was finally settled with a season-long loan to the Tigers, and Paul McShane both dotted down in the first ten minutes of the second-half. Anthony Mullaly finally got the visitors on the board in the 52nd minute, but normal service was resumed on the hour mark as Jake Webster, showcasing his power and effective ball-running that would become the norm throughout the season, added yet another four points to the scoreboard. Both Gale and captain, Michael Shenton got in on the act in the final ten minutes courtesy of exhilarating attacking play and spineless defending whilst Joel Moon added a consolation score, cheered ironically by the home fans, two minutes from time.

The Tigers had inflicted one of Leeds' heaviest defeats in history. A 71-0 hammering at the hands of Wakefield Trinity 72 years ago was the last time the Rhinos had been disgraced in such a fashion and it was a victory that the Castleford fans could not quite believe. In Super League, results such as these had more often than not been inflicted upon the Tigers.

From this moment on, it was evident that Castleford were going to do something special as Powell had challenged his players to do before the season started. It was also a victory that shocked Super League teams to the core; the Tigers were well and truly contenders.

WHAT THE FANS SAID

@durhamtiger48: "When Steve Gill picked Sweet Caroline, even he didn't know how true the words were going to be. The very best times in my life."

@jason_ridgway: "what a time to be a Cas fan, unbelievable and there's more improvement to come."

@Becky_Norton: "End of last season losing Denny & Dorn was gutting. Then comes along @GregEden1 & @zakhardaker1 taking 2017 by storm."

@BizarreRl: "What a beautiful display of rugby league all over the pitch. You absolute beauties."

@becky_allatt: "Fantastic game!! Classy Cas were on fire."

#4 - Michael Shenton

Date of Birth: 22/07/1986
Height: 190cm (6 ft 2)
Weight: 93kg (14.6 stone)
Country: England
Position: Centre
Previous Clubs: St Helens
National Honours: 9 caps for England

Appearances: 26	**Avg. Gain:** 7.35
Tries: 6	**Tackles:** 382
Try Assists: 19	**Clean Breaks:** 14
Metres: 1719	**Offloads:** 12

After being sidelined for the whole of the 2016 season courtesy of a horrendous injury sustained in the 2016 opener against Hull KR, Shenton bounced back in 2017 to lead his team to record-breaking achievements. 'Captain Fantastic' is how Shenton should be known for the starring role he played for the Tigers in 2017. Michael's capabilities were shown to a hugely impressive level and these were duly rewarded with his inclusion in the 2017 Super League Dream Team. His truly wonderful attacking skill and the tight link-up plays with Luke Gale and Zak Hardaker were responsible for so many of Greg Eden's tries down that infamous left-side attack. His magnificent tip-on for Eden's first try in the away hammering of Widnes in March or his even more stupendous no-look flick pass to Eden at the Magic Weekend were just some prominent examples of Michael's ability to stun his audience with unteachable skills. Let's take nothing away from the defensive part of his game though either. His ability to wrap up opponents and stop the play dead is a key facet of Michael's defensive play. And in 2017, his remarkable relationship with Greg Eden was not just an attacking plus, it was also vital to the Tigers' shut-out ability and thus the astounding points difference that Castleford accrued.

A Castleford lad winning and, more importantly, captaining his team to the title seemed surreal for Michael in 2017. The image of him lifting the League Leaders' Shield and walking the team out at Old Trafford will live long not just in Tigers' fans memories, but also in his own, as recollections of the dire straits Castleford have faced in the past were wiped away as he and the team he so proudly led created new and unforgettable history. It was therefore harsh and surprising to see that Michael had not been selected in England's 24-man squad for the World Cup by Wayne Bennett.

@alanwdawson – 14th July 2017: "Michael Shenton is a class act..."

@MikeGlover87 – 18th June 2017: "No better centre in SL than Michael Shenton."

@Robbeezley - 29th May 2017: "@mshenton22 has to be one of the best ever centres in our game, service to Eden and any winger is second to none."

TIGERS TOO HOT FOR THE VIKINGS

Buoyed by their convincing mauling of the Rhinos, Castleford visited the infamous iPitch where teams often struggle. No such problems here as the Tigers confidently dispatched the Cheshire club.

The early stages did, however, prove difficult for the Tigers and only fierce defence kept the Vikings scoreless as they were held up over Cas' line on three occasions. Leigh, Warrington and Leeds had all felt the force of the Tigers' slick attack in spells and Widnes were no exception. Midway through the first half, the Tigers struck four times in a scorching 18 minute period to take the game out of reach for the hosts. First, hooker Paul McShane set up Greg Minikin on the right and just a few minutes later Minikin had his second thanks to a brilliant break by Ben Roberts.

Castleford's left side then got in on the act. Shenton was put through a gap by a great Gale pass and then moments later, Gale again fed Shenton who tipped the ball on magnificently to winger Greg Eden who finished spectacularly in the corner. Gale missed his first conversion of the day, but the Tigers went in 22-0 ahead at the break. The try-scoring procession continued into the second-half as Matt Cook, within minutes of the resumption, showed great determination to force his over and then Eden completed the scoring in the 54th minute following another superb offload by his centre Shenton. As Gale converted both, the mercurial half-back passed 1500 career points with his five goals.

With the scoring ending with 26 minutes left, the hosts tried valiantly to break down the Tigers' defence, but the Castleford defence stood firm. With Widnes failing to register a point, they became the first team since Harlequins in 2009 to be kept scoreless by the Tigers.

A competent display showed just how far the Tigers had come under Powell. Attacking had never been a problem for Castleford, but question marks have always been raised over their ability and desire to defend. On this performance, neither the ability nor the desire to defend could be questioned.

WHAT THE FANS SAID

@Philsno1: "The scoreboard says it all Widnes Vikings 0 Castleford Tigers 34 awesome performance by all 17 @CTRLFC boys I can't wait until Salford game!"

@markcoulthard: "wow it's just like watching Brazil it's just like watching Brazil @CTRLFC #coyf."

@tigeramyh: "What a game #COYF #differentleague."

@Sports_mad_guy: "Seems even the plastic pitch at Widnes can't stop the march of @CTRLFC."

@misskeeleywhite: "Awesome effort by the lads today what an impact @Jnrmoors made he is a machine, great finish also by @GregEden1 #goodtimes #coyf."

#5 - Greg Eden

Date of Birth: 14/11/1990
Height: 181cm (5 ft 9)
Weight: 91kg (14.3 stone)
Country: England
Position: Full-back/Wing
Previous Clubs: Huddersfield Giants, Hull KR, Salford Red Devils, Brisbane Broncos
National Honours: Called up to 27-man England training squad in 2017

Appearances: 29	**Avg. Gain:** 8.30
Tries: 38	**Tackles:** 59
Try Assists: 10	**Clean Breaks:** 47
Metres: 2624	**Offloads:** 19

Greg was initially signed to be the full-back replacement for the outgoing Luke Dorn. However, Zak Hardaker's arrival on a season-long loan from Leeds Rhinos edged Greg out to the wing and he never looked back. A truly astonishing 37 tries in 24 appearances was not just down to the service inside him.

With remarkable pace and an eye for a classy finish, Eden established himself as one of the league's best wingers. The Denny Solomona record of 40 league tries and 42 season tries in 2016 looked certain to be broken. An injury suffered in the home win over Salford stopped him in his tracks but thankfully, it didn't end his season. Greg failed to break Solomona's try-scoring record of 2016 and ended the 2017 season with 38 league tries and 41 season tries. Still, this was an outstanding achievement in his first year back at the club. Greg's attacking ability had never been questioned but he struck a formidable defensive relationship with his centre and captain Michael Shenton.

Once a Castleford fan in the stands, it was an absolute pleasure to welcome back Greg and for him to silence the many doubters he has had throughout his career. The way in which his game developed under Powell was epitomised by his selection in the 2017 Super League Dream Team as well as his inclusion in the England Elite Performance training squad. The England inclusion was a major feat considering that Wayne Bennett, the England coach, had often been critical of Eden whilst he had been at the Brisbane Broncos under Bennett's guidance. The way in which Eden had vastly improved all aspects of his game in just under a year made Bennett's decision to omit Greg from England's 24-man World Cup squad harsh on Eden, especially when considering his impressive try-scoring exploits.

Greg has the talent and now has the confidence to make 2018 even more of a success than 2017 and, perhaps obtain that so far elusive England cap.

 **@JojJojoelle - 23nd June 2017:** "*Rugby League supporters at the start of the season* "Cas are really going to struggle without Denny Solomona." Greg Eden: "Hold my pint…"

UNBEATEN RUN COMES TO AN END AS O'BRIEN DROP-GOAL SINKS THE TIGERS

A wet and gloomy Sunday afternoon at Salford beckoned for the Tigers. After four wins on the trot, morale was high in the Castleford camp. But a dogged Salford display saw Castleford drop their first points of the season.

The Tigers could not get a foothold in the game as Gale was kept quiet whilst Salford's pack bullied the Tigers, not least Ben Murdoch-Masila who tormented the Castleford left-side defence. The visitors, however, were first on the scoresheet as early as the fifth minute when a Gale kick confused Red Devils winger Greg Johnson, and from the resulting mix-up Gale touched down. From this moment on, the Tigers were under the cosh as the hosts piled on the pressure.

The Tigers' defence finally cracked just after the half-hour mark as Salford half-back Robert Lui fed the rampaging Murdoch-Masila who left two defenders in his wake as he trampled his way to the line. The Tigers believed they had scored just before the break after Michael Shenton had sent Greg Eden in at the corner only for it to be pulled back for a dubious forward pass.

The visitors weren't to be denied for long, however. Three minutes after the break, Jake Webster picked up a loose ball and fed Greg Minkin who dragged opposition defenders with him to the try line. Minikin was however injured in the act of scoring and subsequently had to leave the field. With Webster moving to the wing and McMeeken to centre, Salford ramped up the intensity and in the 54th minute, Murdoch-Masila got his second after juggling with the ball and charging his way to the line 15 metres out. Gareth O'Brien converted and then added a penalty in the 67th minute following a Castleford infringement. As Webster was also forced to exit the field through concussion minutes later, Hardaker now occupied the wing spot with Roberts at full-back and McShane at half back, leaving the game 12-12 but it was advantage Salford as it entered the final stages. Both sides went toe-to-toe, but it was the hosts who took the lead after Eden fumbled the ball inside his own half. Red Devils fullback Gareth O'Brien was on hand to slot the winning drop-goal in the 77th minute, much to the agony of the travelling fans.

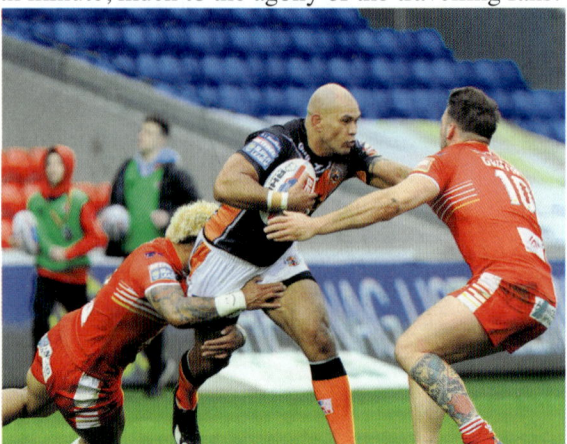

It was certainly a drop back down to earth for the Tigers fans after the seemingly unstoppable Castleford bandwagon had started off so well. It was also clear to Powell that his team would need to adapt to more slippery conditions and a bullying pack. Certainly, later results such as the away victory at Wigan in April and the dominant display against Salford in the Super 8s would highlight how the Tigers had improved in such conditions from this disappointing performance.

WHAT THE FANS SAID

@charlotteroseg_: "Fair play Salford completely shut our game down. Onwards to next week at home."

@jacks1973_66835: "Can't win them all. It's how we respond next week, onwards and upwards."

@GoProJonny: "Back to earth with a bump. To everyone looking ahead to the Wigan game next month, this was what I expected. Frustrating result."

@jonny_binns: "Not ideal but maybe what we need. A tight fought, tough game, rather than just scoring for fun. Need to be tested at some point."

@lee46b: "Hate Cas losing but Salford's game plan really worked. Now time to see how Cas come back from it, roll on Sunday against Catalans."

#6 - Rangi Chase

Date of Birth: 11/04/1986
Height: 171cm (5 ft 6)
Weight: 88kg (13.8 stone)
Country: New Zealand/England
Position: Stand-off
Previous Clubs: Wests Tigers, St George Illawarra Dragons, Salford Red Devils, Leigh Centurions
National Honours: 2 caps for New Zealand Maori, 8 for England

Appearances: 8	**Avg. Gain:** 7.15
Tries: 0	**Tackles:** 48
Try Assists: 4	**Clean Breaks:** 0
Metres: 279	**Offloads:** 2

Having left Castleford at the end of the 2013 season, in a high-profile and controversial move to the newly-rebranded Salford Red Devils, it was clear Rangi had some making up to do to the fans whom once cherished him. Returning in July 2016 to the club he claimed to have "fallen in love with", most Tigers fans welcomed him back with open arms.

Powell gave Chase the number 6 shirt going into the 2017 season ahead of Ben Roberts. In the opening two matches, the loyalty was repaid as Chase combined masterfully with half-back partner Luke Gale to inflict defeat on both Leigh Centurions and Warrington Wolves. However, trouble was never far away from Rangi, and before Castleford played host to Leeds Rhinos, he was suspended by the club after an internal investigation. Rangi would only return when Powell, rightly, had seen enough commitment and determination from Chase in training to force himself back into contention. It wasn't until three games after the Leeds clash that Rangi made a small cameo off the bench against Catalans Dragons. The mercurial talent was on the bench a week later and showed glimpses of the class that Castleford fans had once lapped up when he set up Joel Monaghan for two tries in Castleford's pummelling of Huddersfield.

After this, Rangi would make four more appearances his last being away at Huddersfield where he was taken off injured. Unfortunately, Rangi let his private indiscretions run amok and was again the subject of an internal investigation which eventually saw him leave the club on loan to Widnes in May and then permanently in July. In August 2017, it was announced that Rangi had tested positive for cocaine, leading to his suspension by the Vikings. Unplayable on his day, it was incredibly sad to witness the decline of such an envious talent.

@PaddyL1996 – 3rd August 2017: "Rangi Chase seems like a decent bloke and he could've been one of the best rugby league players in the country. Such a shame."

@TheGameCaller – 31st March 2017: "Cas v Hudd tonight will be remembered for some mercurial magic from the Rangi Chase. Simply sensational Rugby League - watch the highlights."

THE TIGERS EXTINGUISH THE DRAGONS' EARLY FIRE TO RECLAIM TOP SPOT

It was necessary for Castleford to rally after the disappointment of their first loss of the season in the previous week at Salford. And they did so, even after they trailed 14-0 ten minutes into the first-half. Iain Thornley crossed for the visitors in the third minute following a Ben Roberts mistake. Then four minutes later, Richie Myler was the beneficiary of a well-timed Paul Aiton pass to extend the lead. Luke Walsh improved both and then added a penalty to send the Dragons into a big unlikely lead.

Zak Hardaker, however, responded for the Tigers with their first foray into the visitors' half on 13 minutes. With substitutes Junior Moors and Grant Millington injecting life into the Tigers, the home side quickly turned the screw. The Tigers, who appeared to be suffering somewhat of a hangover from the disappointment at Salford, scored three tries in 11 minutes as Millington, Joel Monaghan and Greg Eden all crossed the whitewash much to the delight of the expectant Mend-a-Hose Jungle. Eden's try on 36 minutes was particularly impressive, coming from a scrum won against the head, a feat relatively unseen in the modern game. With Gale missing only one conversion, the Tigers were up 22-14 at the break which was a stunning turnaround from the opening stages of the game and yet more evidence of the Tigers' ability to turn the screw rapidly and exuberantly.

Although the Dragons scored the first try of the second-half just a minute in as Louis Anderson barged his way over, it was largely one-way traffic after the break. Moors went through a glaring gap in the Catalans' defence on 46 minutes and, just before the hour mark, skipper Michael Shenton scored a delightful try after taking a return pass from Eden after the former had started the move deep inside the Tigers half. The game was drifting away from the visitors as Gale added to both conversions with a drop-goal on 63 minutes to stretch Castleford's lead to 37-20. Then Eden jinked his way over three minutes later to inflate the scoreline even further.

Having scored 21 unanswered points to push Catalans out of sight, Castleford did concede

in the final ten minutes as Vincent Duport took a neat pass to finish in the corner. With Luke Walsh converting five from five, the game finished 43-26 in favour of the hosts. This was far from a complete performance. Indeed Castleford would only concede five tries in four other games: March's game away at Warrington, the Super 8s and semi-final games at home to St Helens and the Super 8s defeat to Hull.

This victory was just what the Tigers needed after succumbing to their first defeat the previous week. With exciting attacking play on show once more and an overwhelming spell of Castleford flair midway through the first half, the Tigers reclaimed top spot and inflicted a fourth defeat in four for the struggling Dragons.

WHAT THE FANS SAID

@danielskinner91: "I would've snatched your hand off if you'd offered me that result after the first 15 mins. I'm happy with that."

@SeanWilson85: "A tough, scrappy game. Could have gotten away from us. Showed good composure to get back in and take control."

@underwood_81: "Dirty, scrappy game, poorly officiated but after giving 14 start I guess it's not a bad result. Improvement needed, onwards & upwards."

@jodi_1991: "Not at our best there but got the 2 points and we're top of the league!!!!"

@Garethvicar: "Considering that start and questionable refereeing I'll take that scoreline."

#7 - Luke Gale

Date of Birth: 22/06/1988
Height: 180cm (5 ft 9)
Weight: 85kg (13.4 stone)
Country: England
Position: Scrum-half
Previous Clubs: Doncaster, Harlequins RL, Bradford Bulls
National Honours: 3 caps for England Knights, 3 caps for England

Appearances: 28	**Avg. Gain:** 5.78
Tries: 14	**Tackles:** 304
Try Assists: 21	**Clean Breaks:** 8
Metres: 815	**Offloads:** 9

2017 was a step up for Luke Gale. Orchestrating the Tigers on the field, Gale consolidated his position as the best half-back in the country, and it was no shock to see him included in the 24-man England World Cup squad. His link-up play with Zak Hardaker and Michael Shenton in the Tigers' devastating left-side attack put fear into the hearts of the Tigers' opponents Whilst his boot saw him notch up the most conversions, 40/20s and drop goals in the league (130, ten and nine respectively). His hat-tricks in the thrashings of Leeds and Huddersfield at home were just rewards for an immaculate talent that always seems to be backing up breaks or directing his team around the field.

His 2017 points tally was an emphatic one as Luke smashed his own record for the second year running for most goals kicked in a Castleford season as well as ending the 33-year reign of Bob Beardmore's overall points tally in a season. Luke again made history in 2017 by becoming the first player to win the Albert Goldthorpe Medal three years in a row whilst he also appeared in the Super League Dream Team for a third successive year, further epitomising his consistency and importance for the Tigers since his arrival. To add yet another accolade to his impressive 2017 collection, Luke received the Rugby League Writers and Broadcasters Association Player of the Year. Luke was not finished there, he became only the fourth Castleford player to win the Man of Steel, chosen by his peers for his performances in 2017.

Luke was however taken ill in early September with appendicitis, a cruel twist of fate. It was uncertain whether Gale would appear again for the Tigers in 2017. But Gale, just 16 days after his operation, took his place on the field in the semi-final against St Helens, playing arguably one of his greatest games in a Tigers shirt to propel the Tigers to Old Trafford for the first time in their history. A cool last-minute penalty to take the semi-final into golden-point and then a wonderful drop-goal in extra-time firmly etched Luke into Castleford folklore.

@webbez – 11th August 2017: "Luke Gale the last of the maverick half backs such as Long, Goulding and Gregory amongst others before him."

@Fatboy_Rob – 22nd July 2017: "Luke Gale: Man of the decade. Never mind Man of Steel!"

THE TIGERS MAUL THE GIANTS IN EMPHATIC FASHION

Both Luke Gale, on his 250th career appearance, and Joel Monaghan registered hat-tricks as Castleford thumped struggling Huddersfield. Despite Ryan Hinchcliffe opening the scoring for the Giants in the seventh minute after he twisted through some weak defence, the match became a one-sided affair.

Buoyed by their victory over Catalans the previous week, the Tigers never looked like losing after grabbing a hold of the game to go in 16-4 at the break. Ben Roberts touched down from a Gale kick in the 19th minute and then he turned provider for Jake Webster to crash over just three minutes later. Again in customary fashion, yet another devastating short period of Tigers dominance was finished as Mike McMeeken took a nice Paul McShane pass to crash over through some frail defending in the 27th minute. Gale missed the kick for Webster's try but converted the other two to make it 16-4.

With many wasted chances, not least by winger Greg Eden who could have had a first-half hat-trick to his name, the Giants were lucky to be only down by 12 points as the teams left the field. Eden made up for his earlier errors and, by the 43rd minute, the contest was effectively over after both Gale, who was supplied with a timely pass by Eden after the winger had made an excellent break deep in his own half, and Milner, who dummied his way expertly to the line, scored within two minutes of each other.

Brief respite for the Giants came through Ryan Brierley just before the 50th minute as he raced 80 metres from a scrum. This proved to be only a momentary break from the onslaught which greeted the Giants' line. Four minutes after Brierley's effort, Gale had his 100th career try courtesy of a neat Webster pass who then put in Monaghan for his first of the night. Gale got his hat-trick on 57 minutes after good work by Paul McShane

69

and then trickster Rangi Chase, in his first game back after being dropped for disciplinary issues before the Leeds game in March, provided magic that has not been seen enough in the past few years to get Monaghan over for his second.

Lee Gaskell got Huddersfield's third and final try approaching the 70th minute, pouncing on a Brierley kick. But fittingly, Castleford had the final word as Monaghan recorded his hat-trick after a perfectly weighted Chase kick with just three minutes remaining.

Orchestrating the play, and at times mesmerising the Giants' defence, with a 24-point haul and with him surpassing 100 career tries in his 250th career appearance, Luke Gale firmly established himself as the frontrunner for the end of season prize, the Man of Steel. The only negative to his performance was his unusually inaccurate goal-kicking as he missed four from ten. The Giants were simply blown away by a red-hot Castleford side that were living up to their pre-season hype. The Tigers were however still leaking silly points and the ability to keep switched on for 80 minutes would be severely tested in the trip to Wigan six days later.

WHAT THE FANS SAID

@presh53_ruth: "We are tremendous! No atmosphere in Super League like the Jungle! Brilliant players, coaches, board and fans! Just saying!

@KTate07: "That @ CTRLFC points difference at the top of the league is ridiculous. Well played lads. Keep grinding keep winning."

@MarcRayne: "Scrappy in places however scored some brilliant tries...we are top of the league #COYF."

@tigeramyh: "I made it all the way from Coventry to get to the @CTRLFC I'm so pleased. Amazing work #COYF #differentleague #topoftheleague

@MJE_1982: "Almost 35 years old and never been to a rugby league match in my life until tonight @CTRLFC loved it, I'll be back!"

AVERAGE
APRIL

#8 - Andy Lynch

Date of Birth: 20/10/1979
Height: 187cm (6 ft 1)
Weight: 102kg (16.1 stone)
Country: England
Position: Prop
Previous Clubs: Bradford Bulls, Hull FC
National Honours: 5 caps for England,
1 cap for Great Britain

Appearances: 19	**Avg. Gain:** 7.27
Tries: 0	**Tackles:** 392
Try Assists: 0	**Clean Breaks:** 2
Metres: 1519	**Offloads:** 3

38 years old by the time he retired, Andy has been a cornerstone of the game. And in 2017, the prop forward joined the elusive '500 club' as he became only the seventh player ever to make 500 career appearances. At the start of the 2016 season, Lynch also became the oldest player in Super League with Jamie Peacock retiring.

Andy is well-known for his effort in training and the experience he gives the Tigers behind the scenes. Although Andy played a smaller role on the field in 2017, often appearing off the bench for little more than ten or twenty-minute cameos, the winning culture he inspired was witnessed throughout the team as a whole. The lack of game-time was perhaps warranted as a severe leg break in the 2016 season, which saw him play only 12 games that year, was hardly conducive for a prop nearly hitting 40 years of age. Powell used Lynch commendably in 2017; it was evident that Andy could not play week-in-week-out and was often marred by injury. Selected matches throughout the season enabled the veteran to become the second highest ranked player for Super League appearances and just saw him miss out on Kevin Sinfield's total of 434.

Retiring from the game, Andy bowed out having made impressive individual history, but fittingly, he also ended his career in what was a memorable season with his hometown club. All youngsters that play the sport need a role model to whom they can look up. Lynch certainly fits the bill; a keen and humble family-man, a vocal enforcer whilst on the pitch, and with a work ethic that is second to none. Andy is the pinnacle of what a Rugby League player should be. It is also fantastic to see that Andy will become the club's Welfare Officer in 2018, a fitting role for a person that has gone through all of the sport's ups and downs.

@boylebags19 – 5th October 2017: "Fantastic servant to rugby league. Always set the standards both on and off the field! One of the toughest most durable players to play the game #respect #leader #rolemodel @8AndyLynch."

@TBones49 – 17th August 2017: "A great player and a great ambassador for the club and for rugby league. I'm sure you'll make a success of whatever comes next."

TENACIOUS TIGERS RECORD STUNNING VICTORY

With attacking panache on show in the previous two weeks, this fixture demanded defensive steel from the Tigers against a patched-up Wigan side. Daryl Powell could hardly have been disappointed as the visitors restricted their hosts to just a try in either half, both courtesy of impressive full-back Morgan Escare.

The prospect of an away victory was dampened before kick-off as influential captain Michael Shenton pulled up with a back injury sustained in the warm-up. Joel Monaghan was drafted into the side in a last-minute re-shuffle, with Greg Minikin switching to centre after returning from a two-match injury absence.

This late change appeared to affect the Tigers as they made a slow start. Three handling errors inside the opening ten minutes allowed Wigan to pile on the pressure. But the Tigers showed their grit to come out the other side and register the first points of the evening with two tries in three minutes. First, Jake Webster took advantage of a wonderful Ben Roberts pass to slide over in the 24th minute and then Luke Gale supported fullback Zak Hardaker through the middle of the field following a wonderful offload by the increasingly impressive Jesse Sene-Lefao. Gale converted both and added a penalty six minutes later to increase the visitors' lead to 14-0.

The Tigers would have been disappointed to let in a try just five minutes before the break as speedster Escare rounded Luke Gale to post Wigan's first points. His own conversion attempt was wayward and the scores remained 4-14 at half-time. Just three minutes into the second-half, up stepped Sene-Lefao, by now becoming a joy to watch and just have around the club for Castleford. After taking a well-timed Paul McShane pass, the popular

73

Samoan shook off four defenders to rampage through the Warriors defence to score a memorable try, much to the joy of the Tigers fans behind the posts. Gale added the two from in front of the posts and the Tigers had a lead of 20-4 and it would stay this way for half an hour before Escare got his second after a great break by Wigan winger Tom Davies.

The hosts continued to apply the pressure going into the last five minutes of the game and appeared to be within a sniff of a comeback when an attempted pass to Davies by Joel Tomkins was swooped upon by Greg Eden. The former Brisbane Bronco raced nearly 100 metres to end the contest and send the travelling black-and-amber army home ecstatic.

A superb victory showed the rest of Super League that the Tigers were

not just a fancy attacking team, but that they had the guts and determination to defend their line admirably. With seven wins from eight, Castleford were really lighting up the league and demonstrating that they were the team to beat. Wakefield, the Tigers' archrivals, would be the next to try.

WHAT THE FANS SAID

@CasTigers_RL: "I have never ever seen Cas play with that kind of defence! Incredible."

@hirsty: "So proud of you @CTRLFC boys. I'm slowly converting the London banking cyber security teams to be Cas fans. Brilliant advert!"

@Scottoconnor: "If anyone's looking for George Williams have a look in @ben02roberts back pocket he seems to have been there most of the night."

@Caron4: Well done to @CTRLFC great win and what you feeding @ AdzMilner – he's absolutely awesome. Great team performance and shout to @ ben02roberts."

#9 - Paul McShane

Date of Birth: 19/11/1989
Height: 167cm (5 ft 5)
Weight: 91kg (14.3 stone)
Country: England
Position: Hooker
Previous Clubs: Leeds Rhinos, Hull FC,
Widnes Vikings, Wakefield Trinity
National Honours: Called up to 27-man
England training squad in 2017

Appearances: 31	**Avg. Gain:** 6.63
Tries: 3	**Tackles:** 892
Try Assists: 21	**Clean Breaks:** 6
Metres: 1001	**Offloads:** 13

After struggling to find a consistent home, Paul McShane found a home at the Tigers. His skill set and rugby brain are amongst the best in the competition, whilst he never shies away from defensive work or even roughing it with the so-called 'big boys'. In 2017,

Paul, like so many of his teammates, found an extra gear, so much so that he was called up to the England Elite Performance Squad, but surprisingly missed out on both a World Cup and Dream Team place.

Paul's reading and understanding of the game are so great that, in 2016 and 2017, he was often called in to deputise in the halves in the absence of Rangi Chase, Ben Roberts or Luke Gale. In fact, in two of Castleford's most impressive performances in 2017, the home drubbing of Leeds in March and the astounding win at Wigan in September, McShane found himself partnering Luke Gale and Jake Trueman respectively in the halves.

Paul's decision-making and crisp passing from acting half was such a vital factor in the much-raved about attacking flair which the Tigers exhibited throughout the season as he provided Gale and Roberts with the platform and the time from which to launch their devastating attacks. Moreover, Paul's kicking game out of dummy half took on a new level in 2017. Whilst defenders were scrambling out of the line to get to Gale or Roberts, McShane added another dimension to the Tigers' attack with his accurate boot, recording two 40/20s and numerous tactical kicks. And when Gale was absent Paul took over the goalkicking duties to great effect and in doing so, notched up 34 points with the boot.

Never one to take a backwards step, Paul is in the mould of the hookers of old: Intelligent and, despite his small stature, aggressive. He is a player loved by his teammates, loathed by his opponents, and one Castleford fans never got sick of seeing in 2017.

2018 promises even more from Paul and if he delivers, that England cap that 2017 could have yielded cannot be far away.

@expressbrandbiz – 10th October 2017: "@mcshane_paul...54 Grand Final tackles made, the man is a machine and if anybody think he hasn't been the best hooker of 2017 they are barmy."

TRINITY BRUSHED ASIDE WITH EASE BY IMPRESSIVE TIGERS

A feisty local derby awaited at the Mend-a-Hose Jungle for the first game in the often criticised Easter period. This was a fixture that saw Andy Lynch rise to second in the all-time Super League appearances chart, as he notched up his 440th game to move clear of St Helens stalwart Paul Wellens.

Castleford started the slower of the two teams allowing David Fifita to barge over from close range after the Tigers had failed to deal with a towering kick in just the third minute. But the Tigers soon clicked into gear as Ben Roberts, arcing his run around the Trinity defence after a neat run around play with Mike McMeeken, and Jake Webster, fed by a Roberts pass, scored within two minutes of each other to turn the game on its head. Four more first-half tries were to come for the Tigers as Oliver Holmes crossed for his first of the season thanks to a Luke Gale pass before prop Grant Millington showed classy footwork for both of his four-pointers on 28 and 34 minutes respectively. Prior to Millington's second try, Bill Tupou had responded for the visitors with a great catch from yet another Wakefield kick. But with three minutes to go until a half-time breather, Webster got his second to put the Tigers out of sight.

The first-half had been frenetic and fast and unsurprisingly, the second was a much slower affair. Up 36-12 at the break, Castleford took their foot off the gas in the second 40 minutes, scoring only one further try through Greg Eden. Fifita grabbed his second 15 minutes into the second-half and Ben Jones-Bishop scored with another spectacular winger's finish four minutes before the end, but Castleford ran out comfortable winners.

In emphatic fashion, the Tigers secured the Adam Watene trophy, a prize in memory of the late prop-forward who played for both clubs before his tragic death in 2008, aged 31. Castleford would need to improve especially in defence, as so often had been the case in the opening nine rounds, as two away games at St Helens and Hull FC beckoned within the space of six days.

WHAT THE FANS SAID

@CallumLand: "Grant Millington is unreal, it's not till you watch a game back that you appreciate just what he does."

@rosshardyyork: "#COYF well I assume that second half was us just keeping fresh for Monday. Still top, 2 more points, happy."

@danielskinner91: "Fizzled out towards the end but a good win that, trin are a good side. Onwards & upwards. #coyf."

@nathastbury: "I think that the results are important than the performance over Easter. My man of the match had to be @ben02roberts, awesome again."

@JakeMaw: "Better to have an ugly win than a pretty loss! 2points in the right direction!! #SweetCaroline #coyf."

#10 - Grant Millington

Date of Birth: 1/11/1986
Height: 193cm (6 ft 3)
Weight: 110kg (17.3 stone)
Country: Australia
Position: Prop/Second Row/Loose Forward (just about anywhere, full-back anyone?)
Previous Clubs: Cronulla Sharks, Canterbury Bulldogs

Appearances: 28	**Avg. Gain:** 6.14
Tries: 6	**Tackles:** 732
Try Assists: 5	**Clean Breaks:** 4
Metres: 2129	**Offloads:** 25

Grant is a half-back in a prop's body. Nothing gave greater evidence of this than 2017. Grant's skill set is also second to none and he has such delicate poise for someone of his size. His two tries versus Wakefield in April demonstrated his neat footwork as he stepped past at least two defenders for both of his tries.

In August, Grant, to the delight of the Castleford fans, signed a new one-year extension to the five-year deal he signed in 2014 which will see him a Tigers player until at least 2020. This was another statement from the club as teams are built around people like Grant. He has driven the standards and the culture of the club since his arrival in 2012 and has been integral to the way Castleford have played in recent seasons, especially in 2017. It is no coincidence that the Tigers seem to lift their game whenever Grant is on the field, a feature that became more evident in 2017. The impact he had off the bench was remarkable. He lifted not only his fellow players but the crowd, creating an air of ascendancy that so often left the Tigers in control.

He has a rugby brain like no other prop in Super League, so much so that he actually deputised at half-back when he was called upon in 2016 as Castleford succumbed to an ever-increasing injury crisis. A place in the 2017 Super League Dream Team finally saw him given warranted recognition. Yet amongst the Tigers supporters, he is lauded as being amongst the very best southern hemisphere recruits and is often spoken of in the same sentence as Adrian Vowles in that respect.

The word legend gets bandied about rather too often, but for Castleford, Grant epitomises the definition. There seems to be little left on which Grant can improve for 2018, but all Castleford fans know he will somehow step up his game even further.

@dannylund889011 – 23rd August 2017: "One of our finest imports in our 91 year history @G_Millington_ well earned new contract, we're a different team with you out there!"
@TommyNewbould – 18th August 2017: "Grant Millington could possibly be the best forward we've ever had at Cas, absolute quality."

TIGERS EXTEND LOSING RUN AT ST HELENS TO 23 YEARS

After finally breaking the hoodoo of failing to win at St Helens for over 20 years in a pre-season friendly, Castleford could not perform in the league game that mattered as Jamahl Lolesi obtained his first win as interim coach for the Saints.

Both sides rotated very little despite the short Easter turnaround and Saints seemed to handle the fatigue a little better, although it was the Tigers who stormed into an 8-0 lead through yet another Greg Eden try and a Luke Gale conversion and penalty. However, three tries in ten minutes, all converted by the instrumental Mark Percival who also added a penalty, put the hosts well in contention to inflict the Tigers' second defeat of the season. The Tigers, however, determined to claw their way back into the contest, rallied after the break with Ben Roberts scoring a fine individual try just five minutes in. The conversion having been nailed by Gale, the visitors had brought the game back to a six-point ballgame, with the Saints up 20-14. The Tigers reduced the deficit further as the hour mark approached through a scintillating score that saw the Tigers shift the ball from left to right and then finally back to the left for Eden to score in the corner. Gale's missed kick saw the Tigers trail by two.

The comeback fell flat however as Saints put the game to bed with a Regan Grace try in the corner with just 12 minutes remaining. Roberts did manage another try right on the hooter, again demonstrating his power and skill to bounce off three defenders, but it was too late.

A disappointing result for the Tigers saw them succumb to only their second defeat of the campaign.Both Knowsley Road and Saints' new home, now named the Totally Wicked Stadium, have never been happy hunting grounds for Castleford teams, as this gloomy Sunday afternoon proved. 1990 was the last time the Tigers won a league game at St

Helens and they never really looked like destroying this record despite the end result being close. Something had just not clicked for the Tigers on this day, perhaps it was fatigue, perhaps it was the mindset of never winning an away league game at Saints since 1990, perhaps Saints were too strong, but things would not get any easier for Castleford. An enormous clash with Hull FC would follow just six days later.

WHAT THE FANS SAID

@KTate07: "Some Cas fans need to give their head a shake. All doom and gloom after Salford but we turned it around. Can't win every game. Onto Hull."

@SeanWilson85: "If you expect to win every game you'll inevitably be disappointed. Tough place to go as we well know. Roll on next round."

@BizarreRl: "Hey, all teams lose, good teams don't lose by much. Both our losses have been away and by a total of 5 points. Still top, live & learn."

@RossWilliams_: "Disappointing to lose again at Saints but we're still in a great spot going into Hull on Sunday. I look forward to the bounce back."

@Mk_FRugby: "The positive thing out of our defeats is that we aren't getting wiped. Narrow margins."

#11 - Oliver Holmes

Date of Birth: 07/08/1992
Height: 182cm (5 ft 10)
Weight: 97kg (15.3 stone)
Country: England
Position: Second-Row

Appearances: 10	**Avg. Gain:** 5.97
Tries: 1	**Tackles:** 221
Try Assists: 0	**Clean Breaks:** 3
Metres: 376	**Offloads:** 4

It was disappointing to see Oli fail to play the first six games of 2017 following a serious knee injury sustained at the end of 2016. He managed to register only five appearances until a recurrence of the knee injury he suffered in pre-season resurfaced. Holmes went on to miss an even bigger chunk of 2017, not playing in 14 league and cup games, and only made his next appearance in the home loss to St Helens in Castleford's first Super 8s game in early August. Unfortunately for Oli, he would play only another three matches before he was sidelined by a groin problem for another two games.

Oli did, however, play a starring role in Castleford's historic victory over Wakefield Trinity to secure the League Leaders' Shield. This was a fantastic moment for the Castleford born-and-bred back-rower, who despite only being 25 years of age, has been in the Tigers' senior squad for eight years, debuting at just 17 years of age. Although only sporadically wearing the jersey in 2017, when Oli was on the field his presence was duly felt. Known for his impressive tackling ability, he was regularly seen enforcing himself in defence. In rounds 25 and 26 before Oli was sidelined once again, he made 37 and 33 tackles respectively, ranking second in the team overall.

When Holmes is fit, the defensive side to his game is huge for the Tigers. However Holmes also demonstrated his attacking capabilities in the games he did play, often hitting brilliant lines. Even after succumbing to such a horrendous injury, an operation to remove fragments of bone at the back of his knee tendons, he would not give in and it was pleasing to witness Oli go hammer and tongs for the Tigers badge when he took to the field. Oli returned once more in the remarkable away victory at Wigan in September, but following this game, was again forced out of the side with injury, missing both the Hull FC clash and the semi-final against St Helens.

Oli, determined to play some role for the Tigers towards the business end of the season, did return to play in Castleford's first ever Grand Final appearance, showing up well amidst an overall dismal team performance. Let's not forget that Holmes is only 25; he is nowhere near his end yet.

@SamAngell8 – 7th August 2017: "@Oli_Holmes happy birthday man!! Was great seeing you back on Thursday you were phenomenal as always, have a good day!"

@nathastbury – 2nd August 2017: "Who's this new lad @Oli_Holmes in the squad?? Will be great to see the honey monster back on the pitch and tearing it up!! #oggysgonnagetya."

AIRLIE BIRDS OVERCOME LOSS OF LIAM WATTS TO INFLICT CASTLEFORD'S THIRD DEFEAT OF THE SEASON

After last week's loss at St Helens had ended the Tigers' four-match unbeaten run, Castleford needed to right a few wrongs in this week's fixture against a Black-and-Whites side that had conceded 106 points in their previous two games over the Easter period. But it was the Tigers' defence which came under severe pressure in the opening quarter as Hull raced into an 18-0 lead, courtesy of Scott Taylor and two tries from powerhouse winger Mahe Fonua, with just 13 minutes gone.

Then, a moment of madness by FC prop-forward Liam Watts in the 22nd minute saw him given his marching orders by referee Robert Hicks for a high shot on Tigers half-back Luke Gale, who subsequently had to leave the field. Effectively, this action left the Tigers worse off as Gale, arguably the most instrumental player in a Castleford shirt so far in 2017 would not return for the remainder of the game.

The Tigers finally clawed their way back into the contest with a nice finish by Greg Minikin just a minute after Watts had seen red. Ben Roberts crossed five minutes later with an opportunistic scoot from dummy-half but two missed kicks, the second a shocker in front of the sticks, by Roberts himself, left the Tigers 18-8 down. Marc Sneyd kicked a penalty goal just four minutes before the break for the Airlie Birds, but the Tigers had the last word of a frenetic first-half as Michael Shenton scored following a great break by Roberts inside his own half. A shocking start by the Tigers had been somewhat rectified by the time the hooter sounded as the half-time score was only 20-14 in the home side's favour.

The match was finely poised going into the final quarter and only a Carlos Tuimavave try on 63 minutes finally put the nails in the Tigers' coffin with a late Mike McMeeken try being merely a consolation.

With two defeats in two games, Castleford fans were beginning to worry, whilst many pundits and the Rugby League fraternity continued to point out that the Tigers' bubble had burst and that their slide down the table was inevitable. But despite losing two on the trot, the Tigers had not lost by more than four points. In fact, in Castleford's three losses of the season, the Tigers had lost by a combined margin of just seven points. The following few months would demonstrate that Castleford had learnt the lessons from these tight defeats and were not about to give up their top-of-the-table aspirations. The rest of 2017 would also prove that the Tigers' bubble was unquestionably still floating.

WHAT THE FANS SAID

@pontytiger: "Credit to Hull FC showed loads of desire, their defence was unbelievable."

@CallumLand: "You win some you lose some, when you're top and best team in the league, everyone raises their games, just the way it goes."

@Bradshaw_95: "Despite the loss @ben02roberts you are a pleasure to watch! @Jnrmoors @G_Millington_ keep doing what you do! Absolutely awesome players!"

@t8mwd: "Another loss and still top (just) April was always going to be tough. Let's see what we're made of without Gale for the Wigan match."

@Mk_FRugby: "We lack the ability to build pressure and our starts are really hurting us."

#12 - Mike McMeeken

Date of Birth: 10/05/1994
Height: 196cm (6 ft 4)
Weight: 110kg (17.3 stone)
Country: England
Position: Second-Row
Previous Clubs: London Broncos
National Honours: 1 cap for England

Appearances: 30	**Avg. Gain:** 7.88
Tries: 9	**Tackles:** 726
Try Assists: 11	**Clean Breaks:** 10
Metres: 2717	**Offloads:** 45

The Hampshire-born second rower joined the Tigers for the 2015 season after shining in a terrible season for London Broncos. Mike must surely be attributed as one of the greatest coaching finds in the past decade. Since his move, Mike has developed into one of the most impressive back rowers in the UK. His athletic stature and physical capabilities are enormous considering he is just 23 years of age. Mike was tipped for a place in the England squad in 2016 but unfortunately suffered a broken leg to shatter his dream. This did not stop McMeeken in 2017 however, Mike stood out so much at club level that he was given an England cap against Samoa and did not look out of place in the national setup, so much so that he was given a place in the 24-man squad for the World Cup in November as well as a place in the 2017 Super League Dream Team.

His large frame attracts several defenders and, whilst holding off his opponents, his ability to hold the ball securely in one hand adds yet another dimension to his ever-growing list of attributes, a dangerous offload. 2017 was yet another fine season for the aptly nicknamed 'Big Russian'. It epitomised just how much Mike had polished his game under Powell. His devastating line-running caused teams all sorts of havoc throughout the year. His magnificent break to set Zak Hardaker on his way against Warrington in February and his superb solo effort in the home thrashing of Wigan in late April are just two prominent examples of how Mike was able to punch holes through the opposition line like very few in the game. Not one to shirk from defensive duty, Mike also increasingly revealed his aggressive character in 2017, never shying away from mixing it with opposition forwards as well as battering anyone who ran at him.

Perhaps in the future, the NRL will come calling for his signature and for Mike it will probably be very hard to resist, but in the meantime, Castleford fans can enjoy his presence until at least 2020. And enjoy they will do.

@AdsClobberUK – 17th August 2017: "Mike McMeeken is proof there are genuine quality players in the lower leagues!"
@saralclose – 5th July 2017: "Thrilled with the news about @MMcMeeken94 - fantastic work by @CTRLFC - exciting times!"
@dannylund889011 – 12th June 2017: "Hope we get magic @MMcMeeken94 tied up on a long contract, like until he's 40 or something. Future @CTRLFC & England captain! He's that good!"

TOP-CLASS TIGERS CRUSH THE WARRIORS AFTER SUCCESSIVE DEFEATS

After two successive defeats for the first and only time in 2017, Castleford desperately needed two points to halt their decline in form. What better way to do so than at home against the 2016 champions.

The Tigers hit full throttle from the get-go, registering a first minute try through Adam Milner and racing into a 14-0 lead after Michael Shenton scored from a Zak Hardaker pass and two Luke Gale conversions and a penalty.

Although Sam Powell registered Wigan's first and only points on 25 minutes to cut the gap to 10 points, doing so when Frank-Paul Nuuausala was in the sin-bin, the Tigers always looked in command, registering a half-time score of 26-4 after Matt Cook had forced his way over the line with his first touch of the ball and Mike McMeeken had shown his customary class with a fend on Warriors' scrum-half George Williams and a brilliant run to the line prior to the break.

Half-back Luke Gale needed to pass a head test prior to kick-off to be allowed to play after being knocked to the ground in last week's defeat at Hull FC and, having been passed fit, he gave the Warriors an almighty headache with a 20-point haul, comprising of eight goals and one try.

The procession continued in the second-half as Greg Minikin crossed for his first try of the night just six minutes after the resumption as he took Rangi Chase's exquisite cut-out pass. The stand-off had only come on midway through the first-half in place of the injured Ben Roberts. Luke Gale then played a classy one-two with Grant Millington on 52 minutes for the former to score. More efficient handling saw Jake Webster crash over just five minutes later and Greg Minikin got his second ten minutes from the end after Zak Hardaker sent the final pass.

The Tigers were in such a dominant mood that Daryl Powell was able to bring Gale off despite his head injury clearly not affecting him too badly as he ended with a 100% conversion percentage. That left Paul McShane converting Minikin's last try. Ill-discipline was a constant factor for the Warriors as Morgan Escare and Frank-Paul Nuuausala were

both shown yellow cards for a high-tackle and dissent respectively whilst they also lost three to injury. The Tigers, however, were at their fluid best and showed throughout why expectancy was high at the Mend-a-Hose Jungle in 2017. Taking back top spot, lost following the two defeats to St Helens and Hull FC, the Tigers would not relinquish this position for the remainder of the season. And in dispatching the Warriors with ease in a record-breaking victory (their biggest ever Super League win over Wigan), the Tigers also quelled jibes and criticism that they were not up to the task of continuing their early-season form.

WHAT THE FANS SAID

@MikePreston92: "An 80 minute performance at last! It's all I've wanted for weeks! Top class. Wigan way off the pace but we were outstanding, class defence and the speed in attack was superb."

@GoProJonny: "Possibly one of the most entertaining RL performances I've ever seen. High class rugby and a 50 point win against Wigan… very satisfying!"

@LMacca1: "What a performance last night from cas didn't expect that, good to bounce back #cas #topoftheleague #defence #rugbyleague."

@PhilDransfield: "Love being a Cas fan at the moment!"

@grahamsmithctsc: "AWESOME is the only way to describe that."

MAGICAL
MAY

#13 - Adam Milner

Date of Birth: 19/12/1991
Height: 186cm (6 ft 1)
Weight: 91kg (14.3 stone)
Country: England
Position: Hooker/Loose Forward
National Honours: England Academy
captain

Appearances: 27	**Avg. Gain:** 6.72
Tries: 4	**Tackles:** 779
Try Assists: 2	**Clean Breaks:** 2
Metres: 1317	**Offloads:** 5

Adam joined the club from his local team, Stanley Rangers, and made his first-team debut in 2010. Since then, Adam has grown into one of Castleford's proudest home-grown talents and knows just what 2017 meant to the fans. Prior to the season, Adam was given the number 13 shirt by Powell at the club's shirt launch after impressing in that role towards the back end of 2016 despite always playing hooker in his time with the Tigers beforehand. The decision was an inspired one.

Disregarding his own wellbeing, Adam was seen many a time flying out of the line to stop his often more sizeable opponent and is, more often than not, successful in halting his foe. One can understand why Adam is often on his haunches at the end of games; he is frequently the player leading the line speed and defensive charge. His ball-carrying skills are perhaps unorthodox for the loose forward position, but his toughness, tenacity and willingness to run the ball in as hard as he possibly can has left many of his teammates and Castleford fans questioning why he hasn't been picked for England or included in the 2017 Dream Team. With Paul McShane running the hooking position as good as anyone in 2017, Adam was able to make the loose forward position his own.

Still only 26, 2017 was a year during which Adam blossomed as an enforcer for the Tigers. His commitment to the cause was epitomised in his last-ditch tackle on St Helens' Tommy Makinson in the Tigers' semi-final against St Helens, hauling the winger over the touchline with the try line open. The passion he displays for the badge is a brilliant thing to witness and it was a picturesque moment when Adam was involved in the League Leaders' Shield celebrations and was amongst those walking out at Old Trafford, eleven years after he himself was a ball-boy at Wakefield in 2006 when the Tigers were relegated from Super League.

Players like Adam that have been through thick-and-thin at the club and have witnessed its transformation from the doldrums to a respected and feared fighting force. He deserved to play a great role in the historic 2017 season for sticking by the club through those dark days to the highs of this season.

 **@expressbrandbiz – 15th July 2017:** "Don't think any other human can do the work that @AdzMilner does, he's like a man possessed."

MAMO HAT-TRICK NOT ENOUGH AS CASTLEFORD PREVAIL DESPITE THE LOSS OF KEY MEN

The Tigers went into this game without their England trio of Luke Gale, Zak Hardaker and Mike McMeeken, all of whom had been pivotal to the Tigers' ascent up the table in 2017. Matters were made worse for the Tigers as stand-off Ben Roberts was lost to injury before the game and his replacement, Rangi Chase, was himself injured during the game. With Paul McShane and Tom Holmes in the halves for the majority of the match, Castleford did it tough.

The Tigers started the strongest, taking an eighth-minute lead when Joel Monaghan scored in the corner after slick handling. But then Jake Mamo, who after this game had tallied up six tries in four games after missing the first two months of the season with a broken ankle, grabbed two tries in four minutes. His first in the 19thcame when he backed up Aaron Murphy and his second in the 23rd was a simple finish off a quick play-the-ball. The Aussie would also complete his hat-trick four minutes before the break taking in a clever Danny Brough grubber kick. A Greg Minikin try sandwiched between Mamo's second and third efforts did keep the Tigers on the Giants' tails, but the home side looked in command, leading at the break 18-12.

Just seven minutes into the second-half, the Tigers were level as Greg Eden pounced after good work by Monaghan from a kick. McShane duly converted. Then Castleford were forced to defend ferociously to deny Huddersfield retaking the lead. A Danny Brough drop-goal soon did this however and it took until the 67th minute for the visitors to register another two points courtesy of a McShane penalty. Two minutes later, Castleford were down to 12 men after Jake Webster was sin-binned by referee Ben Thaler for holding down Giants prop Sebastine Ikahihifo despite Webster appearing to snatch the ball one-on-one before the tackle had been completed. Danny Brough, who like Paul McShane ended the night with a perfect goal kicking rate, slotted the resulting penalty between the uprights to put Huddersfield back into the lead at 21-20.

Yet the drama did not end there as Brough himself was sin-binned a few minutes later for a dangerous cannonball tackle. The Tigers made the loss of the Giants' captain pay as Jesse Sene-Lefao, who had an outstanding game, stormed onto a McShane pass to score the match-winning try in the 75th minute. And although the home side peppered the Tigers' line incessantly until the final whistle, they could not breach the stubborn Castleford defence.

Castleford were unrecognisable from the side that thrashed Wigan 54-4 in their previous game but coach Daryl Powell was unsurprisingly delighted with the way they coped without a host of big names. This was a different type of victory for the Tigers: They proved that they could grind out hard-fought wins just as well as they could dance around their opponents with mercurial talent.

WHAT THE FANS SAID

@rossichalm: "Say what you like but that's the biggest win of the season for us! @mcshane_paul massive game and really makes us tick!"

@grahamsmithctsc: "That was a hell of a win tonight. Lots of heart, desire & character, a very important 2 points particularly with key players missing."

@BizarreRl: "Can I just say, @CTRLFC, I love each and every one of you. What a performance under pressure. Great to see a team with such heart and skill."

@CasMarky: "Please @CTRLFC can you stick to scoring 40 points…my nerves can't take that!!!"

@benward001: "Winning big points is good but winning games gritty and battling for every point… that is a TOP TEAM."

CASTLEFORD TROUNCE THE SAINTS TO MARCH INTO THE QUARTER-FINALS

Both sides went straight into the sixth round of the Challenge Cup having finished in the top 8 the previous season. For Saints, the arrival of new coach Justin Holbrook could not have come quick enough. Saints were blown away by a ruthless Castleford side, who left out Rangi Chase following an investigation into his alleged misbehaviour in the week. They had no answer to the free-flowing and exuberant attacking style for which the Tigers became known in 2017.

The danger signs were there early enough for St Helens as the hosts opened the scoring from their first meaningful attack, Scrum-half Luke Gale fed captain Michael Shenton with a fine pass for the first of their 10 tries. Tom Holmes, playing at stand-off in the absence of Chase, then provided the final pass for Jake Webster to register the first of his two tries. Gale kicked the first of his six goals to make it 10-0 after 10 minutes. Fortunately for Saints, Grant Millington was denied another Castleford try for a ball steal and St Helens worked their way back into the game. Centre Ryan Morgan gathered Matty Smith's crossfield kick to touch down midway through the first-half and, shortly after, second-rower Zeb Taia thought he had added another. He was however denied by the video referee who ruled he had grounded the ball short of the line.

This decision was to prove decisive as, instead of being level at 10-10, Saints very quickly found themselves trailing 31-4 after nine minutes of trademark whirlwind rugby from the league leaders. First, Webster got his second following a well-timed Ben Roberts pass. Then just two minutes later, Paul McShane wriggled over from dummy-half and again two minutes later, the Tigers were over once more as Greg Minikin scored the pick of the first-half tries. The winger latched on to a perfect Roberts kick after the latter had made a trademark break. With four minutes to go until half-time, one could have forgiven the Tigers for putting the cue on the rack; but this was the Tigers of 2017: a formidable and determined opponent. Gale slotted over a drop-goal on 39 minutes and on the hooter, Nathan Massey crossed to put the Tigers 27 in front. The break provided some welcome respite for the visitors. Yet normal service was resumed in the second 40 as Eden crossed twice in six minutes and completed

his hat-trick in the 63rd minute. Then the winger on the opposite side, Greg Minikin scored one for the highlights reel as he scorched 70 metres to register his second of the game.

Luke Douglas grabbed a consolation for the Saints with six minutes to go, but it was a rather pitiful afternoon for the visitors against a red-hot Tigers team that welcomed back its three England internationals. The Tigers went into the hat for the quarter-finals of the Challenge Cup in comfortable fashion and were pulled out alongside Hull FC for what would be a titanic clash between two trophy chasing teams.

WHAT THE FANS SAID

@Nooli68: "Yes this year continues to be difficult to believe."

@SeanWilson85: "It's nice to be on the right side of these scorelines after it being the other way for so many years. #COYF."

@Paulctsc: "The magic of the Challenge Cup, classy Cas 2017 style."

@MickTonksT: "What about that 20 minutes of pure brilliance from @ben02roberts. Changed the intensity and direction = job done feet up."

@hewiles: "Unbelievable Cas performance. If there is a better Rugby League team in England, please show me."

#14 - Nathan Massey

Date of Birth: 11/07/1989
Height: 178cm (5 ft 8)
Weight: 99kg (15.6 stone)
Country: England
Position: Loose Forward/Prop

Appearances: 28	**Avg. Gain:** 6.73
Tries: 0	**Tackles:** 589
Try Assists: 0	**Clean Breaks:** 3
Metres: 2133	**Offloads:** 2

When one thinks about the dramatic rise of Castleford Tigers from two relegations to league winners, one thinks of Nathan Massey. Nathan seems to have been at the club forever, making his first-team debut in 2007. Massey has held regular spots in the team ever since, but it is only since Powell came to the club that his ability has been showcased more consistently.

He was rewarded for the significant improvements he had made in 2015 as he signed a four-year deal on the back of some sterling performances. Massey in 2017 hit the form of his life to cement his place in a fiercely competitive squad, whether at prop or at loose forward. Nathan's role in the team is a key one.

Whilst some forwards run the ball in straight and hard, Massey has exceptional skill with his feet to enable him to land on his front and gain a quick play-the-ball, a key weapon. Paul McShane's successful 2017 is definitely reliant on the work of a forward like Massey. Nathan never takes a backwards step in defence and can be seen mixing it with the opponents' pack, despite him being dwarfed by some of his rivals. Nathan is a workhorse and 2017 demonstrated this regularly. He is the type of player that does not get the plaudits, but he is a player that every team needs.

The fact that Nathan has been at the club, just like Adam Milner, through its very dark days to where it is now, made the victory over Wakefield Trinity, the subsequent lifting of the League Leaders' Shield, and the Grand Final appearance even more special. 2018 could well see Nathan improve his game even more; after all, every single season has seen him do just that.

@Craigburbridge1 – 5th October 2017: "Me: Zak's out of the final. Our lass: is @Massey196 still playing? Me: yeah. Our lass: nothing else matters then *mini fist pump* #COYF."

@michellechest68 – 18th August 2017: "Absolute unsung hero this season."

@nathastbury – 17th August 2017: "For a player that's had his critics I imagine it's especially sweet, great to see a player and a fan get his rewards for hard graft."

TIGERS GO TWO POINTS CLEAR AS ST JAMES' PARK PLAYS WITNESS TO A FIRST-CLASS PERFORMANCE

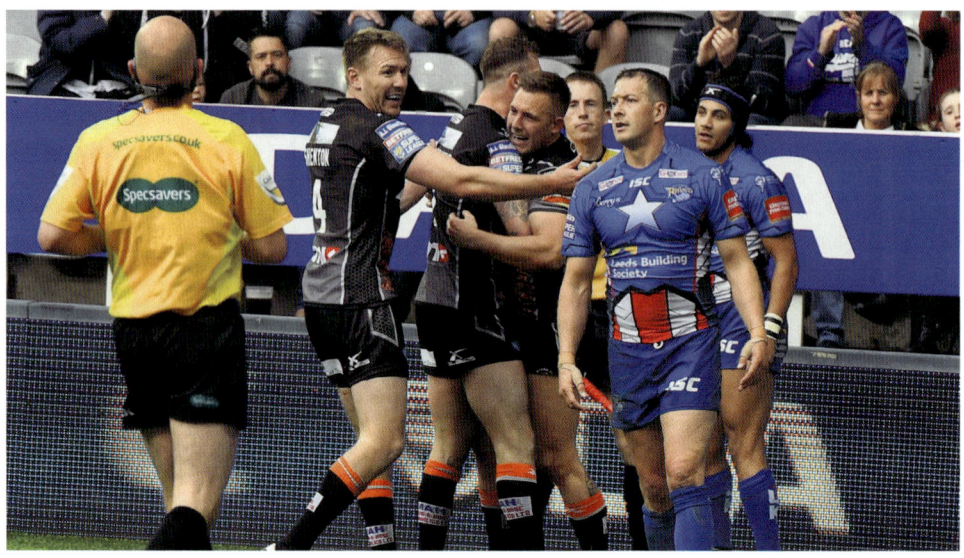

Before the game, Leeds boss Brian McDermott had attempted to rouse his players by challenging his team "to go after" the Tigers after their embarrassing defeat to Castleford in March. This Leeds determination to take the game to the Tigers was quite clear as at half-time, the scores were evenly locked up at 6-6.

Gale crossed in the fourth minute for the Tigers after collecting a knock back by Michael Shenton and Kallum Watkins registered in the 15th for the Rhinos after scorching past his opposite number in Shenton. Wasteful mistakes by Castleford, not least Shenton's wayward pass to Gale with the line beckoning, could have derailed the Tigers. As could the disallowing of a fantastic 'try' by Greg Eden following a planned move at a scrum deep inside the Castleford half by video referee Ben Thaler for an obstruction in the buildup.

But a well-earned breather at half-time seemingly kicked the Tigers back into their stride. Four tries without reply beginning in the 48th minute, including a sensational length-of-the-field effort by young halfback Tom Holmes as well as a hat-trick for Greg Eden, the second of which came courtesy of a wonderful no-look flick pass by his centre, Shenton, put Castleford firmly in the driving seat. And despite two late consolation scores by the Rhinos from Joel Moon and Liam Sutcliffe, after both had taken advantage of soft defending in the 67th and 78th minute respectively, the Tigers had already done the damage in a blistering 15-minute period.

The last match at the Magic Weekend is always the showpiece event and this ferocious West Yorkshire derby did not disappoint. Yet Castleford always seemed one step ahead, seemingly biding their time to unleash the brand of Rugby League for which they had become famous.

For the first time, daylight started to appear between themselves and the rest of the

94

league, as this vital win took the Tigers two points clear at the top. Leeds had definitely improved from their hammering at the Jungle in March, but this was now six times in a row they had failed to beat Powell's Tigers. That figure would become eight by the end of the Super 8s.

WHAT THE FANS SAID

@nogis: "That's a banana skin successful avoided. I was a little worried with some injuries in the first half but they can through in the end #COYF."

@Bulsara_76: "Castleford Tigers. TOP OF THE LEAGUE. Best side in Super League. Awesome."

@misskeeleywhite: "What a fantastic weekend topped off by that super win by the boys today, good to see @zakhardaker1 back fit and great hat-trick by @GregEden1."

@stoner85: "What can I say yesterday was AMAZING cracking day out and the lads pick up another win… Can't wat for next year #COYF @CTRLFC."

@K_Sanderson0304: "So proud of @snozzer_gale at Magic Weekend yesterday!! Brilliant win for Castleford Tigers!! Enjoyed cheering you and the boys on!"

#15 - Jesse Sene-Lefao

Date of Birth: 08/12/1989
Height: 188cm (6 ft 2)
Weight: 108kg (17 stone)
Country: Samoa
Position: Second-row/Prop
Previous Clubs: Manly Sea Eagles,
Cronulla Sharks
National Honours: 2 caps for Samoa

Appearances: 32	**Avg. Gain:** 6.71
Tries: 6	**Tackles:** 679
Try Assists: 2	**Clean Breaks:** 6
Metres: 2779	**Offloads:** 47

Joining for 2017, Jesse was an unknown quantity. But from the moment Castleford fans caught a glimpse of Jesse in the Boxing Day victory over Hull FC, they were besotted with him. 2017 was not just a breakthrough season for the Tigers, it was for Jesse too.

After being only a bit-part squad member for his two previous Australian clubs, Jesse became a pivotal element in the Tigers' historic season as he played in every game of the season whether at prop or second row, the only Tigers player to do so. His commitment and passion on the field was a pure delight to see and the way he fitted into the club, the team and how much he pushed his body to its limit on the field instantly enamoured him to the Tigers supporters. Jesse's blockbusting style and wicked offload was something which had long been missed down at Wheldon Road and his ability to put massive hits on his opponents roused both his teammates and the crowd.

Jesse's highlight reel in 2017 will be full, but one event springs to mind: his try in the away thrashing of Leigh in May when he found himself on the wing on the last tackle. Did the move break down? Not at all! Jesse put in a tremendous grubber kick of which any half-back would have been proud. Luke Gale scooped it up and then fed Jesse with a great offload. Jesse in 2017 will also be remembered for his jovial spirit off the field and how well he interacted with the fans at open days or whenever fans saw him in town.

Always smiling, Jesse brought an energetic buzz to the club which rubbed off on the team, the club and Castleford in general. It will be an absolute pleasure to witness Jesse doing what he does best yet again in 2018: entertaining but also playing with such heart and desire on the field. Jesse is certainly the type of player and person that every club should strive to have and that every player should strive to be. His smile and general approach are infectious whilst his proud religious beliefs demonstrate the respectful and gracious side of Jesse that complements his aggressive and powerful playing style.

@LadyWessie – 14th July 2017: "Bloody love Jesse! He's literally the happiest guy ever! Loves Cas and is proud to wear the shirt...the world needs more Jesses! #COYF."
@SeanWilson85 – 11th June 2017: "Jesse Sene-Lefao is fantastic. Look how happy he was at the end of the game waving to the fans. What a signing. #COYF."

TIGERS SPARED BLUSHES BY LATE RALLY

After the highs of the Magic Weekend and the elation of yet another victory over their big-city rivals, this fixture seemed a mere formality on paper. But on the field, it was anything but as the visitors, whose coach Denis Betts made seven changes from their thrashing at the hands of Wakefield Trinity at the Magic Weekend, defied their lowly league position to give the Tigers a real scare.

When Greg Eden crossed in the 11th minute following a sweeping move from a scrum, it appeared as though the visitors were in trouble. Yet midway through the first half, the Vikings led 12-4 after two great individual tries from winger Ryan Ince in the 19th minute and fullback Jack Johnson in the 27th minute respectively.

As the interval approached, French Guianan prop Gadwin Springer underlined his physical prowess when he barged through the visitors' defence on the 20-metre mark to power over for a much-needed try for the Tigers.

Very few would have predicted a 12-10 scoreline in favour of the Vikings at half-time and even fewer would have expected that by the 50th minute this lead would have grown to 22-10 as Corey Thompson finished spectacularly in the corner and Johnson scored his second through woeful defence.

The shock of going behind further to the team at the bottom of the table kickstarted the Tigers into life and soon, the hosts hit back as stand-off Ben Roberts cleverly put Greg Minikin over in the 54th minute. Four minutes later, Gale's kick to the left corner found the onrushing Eden who somehow managed to juggle the ball whilst in the air and touch it down before he went out of play. Eden then completed his third hat-trick in three games, a truly remarkable feat, when he raced over in the left corner with six minutes remaining and Gale converted. The Mend-a-Hose Jungle then erupted as Matt Cook forced his

97

way over the whitewash late on to confirm another two points for the Tigers albeit in unconvincing circumstances. Yet a few years ago, this would have been a match the Tigers would have lost.

The true sign of a champion team is one that can win 'ugly'. Whilst ugly is a kind word to describe this performance, it was another vital two points that kept up Castleford's momentum at the top of the league. Such an ugly win could well have been justified following the tough encounter against Leeds the week before and just how much the Vikings raised their game, after all, nobody had given them a chance.

WHAT THE FANS SAID

@OliviaPenistonx: "Can't help but feel a little sorry for Widnes, but happy we managed the win."

@saralclose: "In all fairness, apart from some daft mistakes we didn't do much wrong tonight! Widnes came fired up & pushed us all the way! @CTRLFC."

@morsey91: "Widnes deserved the points without a doubt. Tackled their nuts off and scored some decent tries. We were sloppy and complacent."

@Mk_Frugby: "Credit to Widnes. Played really well. Undone by world-class scores. It took that for us to get through them."

@Sports_mad_guy: "Long time since I've seen our fans applaud the away team off at the end, that's how well the Vikings performed."

#16 - Ben Roberts

Date of Birth: 08/07/1985
Height: 173cm (5 ft 8)
Weight: 94kg (14.8 stone)
Country: New Zealand/Samoa
Position: Stand-Off
Previous Clubs: Canterbury Bulldogs, Parramatta Eels, Melbourne Storm
National Honours: 5 caps for New Zealand, 12 caps for Samoa

Appearances: 27	**Avg. Gain:** 8.29
Tries: 10	**Tackles:** 414
Try Assists: 12	**Clean Breaks:** 20
Metres: 2246	**Offloads:** 12

Ben came to the club ahead of the 2015 season from NRL side Melbourne Storm. He took his time to settle in but made his breakthrough with a last-minute drop-goal at home to St Helens in June 2015, the Tigers' first victory against the Saints for seven years. Ben has played a number of positions for Castleford over the years: fullback, stand-off and hooker. His role at stand-off has been integral for the Tigers since he joined the club and his form early in 2016 earned him a contract extension until the end of 2019.

Despite this early-season form, Roberts was injured with a serious foot injury just five days before he signed his contract and would go on to register only one more appearance in 2016. Ben did not let this injury get him down and his 2017 form was seriously impressive, with his silky footwork and classy ball-running being a constant danger for all opposition teams.

Ben's ability to glide across and through the line made him a potent attacking threat for the Tigers that complemented Luke Gale's controlling dominance like no other half-back pairing in the league. Towards the end of 2017, Roberts stoked up a devastating combination down the right with Jake Webster and Mike McMeeken which offered yet another dimension to the Tigers' imposing attack and, whilst the left side rightly won the plaudits, Roberts was key to Greg Minikin's mighty league season haul of 19 tries. Ben, unlike most half-backs in the game, is also a ferocious defender and, often likened to a 'brick wall', he was regularly seen putting an opponent on his backside if he was targeted in the defensive line.

His inventive and formidable play endeared him to the Castleford fans and, at the 2017 awards night in September, Ben received the Fans' Player of the Year which was due recognition for such a pivotal player and person of the Castleford club. Ben was also selected by his country Samoa to play in the 2017 Rugby League World Cup.

@MikePreston92 – 8th September 2017: "Show Benny Roberts a gap and he's gone, best attacking runner in the business at the moment."
@footyfacts37 – 18th August 2017: "Shout out to @CTRLFC for winning the minor premiership. I'd say it's remarkable but when Ben Roberts is round dreams become reality."

EDEN BELIES BELIEF AS CASTLEFORD NIL LEIGH

Another game, another Greg Eden hat-trick. In fact, Eden notched four tries to take his tally to an astonishing 28 tries for the season, just 14 behind the record set by Denny Solomona in 2016 with 14 games to go. Another record tumbled in this game, however: the quickest hat-trick in Super League history and one of the quickest in the history of the sport as Eden crossed three times in a mere five minutes.

Eden's hat-trick added to two efforts from popular forward Jesse Sene-Lefao. His first in the 15th minute resulted from a bizarre and inventive play as Sene-Lefao found himself unmarked down the wing, kicked infield to Luke Gale who returned a pass for the forward to storm over the line. Cas' five tries put the Tigers out of sight by the break with a 28-0 lead. Sene-Lefao's second came eight minutes after his first as he charged onto a Paul McShane pass. With Gale converting both, the Tigers were up 12-0.

Leigh were however seriously unlucky not to have any points on the board as a disallowed Eloi Pelissier try, ruled by video referee Robert Hicks to have been scored via use of prop Antoni Maria as a foil, looked worthy of four points 11 minutes before half-time.

Eden's first try of the day came in the 33rd minute and in messy fashion. Gale was stripped of the ball near the line and Sene-Lefao, at the heart of what the Tigers did well, shipped it out wide to Michael Shenton who fed Eden. Two minutes later, Eden

had his second after a stunning pass from scrum-half Gale who converted. Merely three minutes had passed and Eden had his historic treble, the winger backing up his centre Shenton after a customary Castleford left-side move. Gale converted all but one for the Tigers in the first-half. Another try for Eden ten minutes into the second-half saw the game over as a contest and centre Jake Webster's effort in the 58th minute put the gloss on yet another classy victory.

For the Tigers, however, this match was a costly one. Both Matt Cook, the victim of a nasty cannonball tackle by Leigh's Ben Crooks himself ironically on loan from the Tigers, and Adam Milner were carried off the field with what appeared long-term injuries. The attacking play on show would have pleased Powell tremendously, but the impressive defensive display, nilling a team for the second time in 2017, would have impressed Powell more. After all, he had repeatedly spoken about the need to improve the Tigers' defence. This game was yet another example of how the Tigers now prided themselves on keeping teams out as well as playing remarkable Rugby League.

WHAT THE FANS SAID

@LMacca1: "Good solid result clean sheet, shame about injuries gives other players chance to step up only positive out of a poor negative #Cas."

@danielskinner91: "Proper pleased with that, nilled two teams now! Some great goalline defence on display and some great tries scored. Adz's injury is the only downside."

@Stulake65: "Adz – poss fracture. Cook – medial ligament. Good win but a high price to pay."

@nathastbury: "Jesse Sene-Lefao has just been immense this last month, taken his game to another level, tries, kicks, tackles and runs his blood to water."

@RussGuy74: "Fantastic win from a great @ CTRLFC Cas Tigers team - thanks from all on #Banterbus - you've all made our day."

JUBILANT
JUNE

#17 - Junior Moors

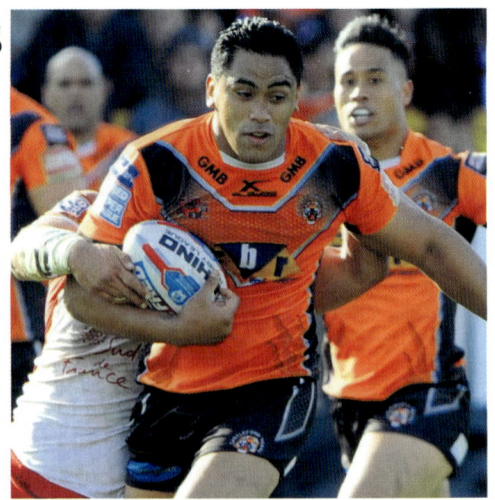

Date of Birth: 30/07/1986
Height: 190cm (6 ft 2)
Weight: 117kg (18.4 stone)
Country: Samoa
Position: Prop/Second-Row
Previous Clubs: Penrith Panthers, Wests
Tigers, Melbourne Storm
National Honours: 3 caps for Samoa

Appearances: 22	**Avg. Gain:** 7.29
Tries: 2	**Tackles:** 471
Try Assists: 4	**Clean Breaks:** 3
Metres: 2385	**Offloads:** 23

Junior arrived in West Yorkshire ahead of the 2015 season from Melbourne Storm with over 50 NRL appearances under his belt. The powerful forward took a while to settle in, but the 2016 season saw Junior establish himself in Super League.

When Junior took to the field in 2017, the impact was obvious; the crowd rose in anticipation as his incredible strength and direct running caused opponents endless problems. Junior has however been plagued by injury over the years and 2017 was unfortunately no different. He missed eight games with a serious knee injury sustained in June's win over Warrington and two with a cheek problem in September. His absence in the cup defeat at Hull was glaringly obvious and for the next seven games, his impact was sorely missed.

Nevertheless, Junior played a vital role for the Tigers in 2017, so much so that he was tipped to be a contender for the Man of Steel award before his eight-game layoff. His size and power provided the hard yards from which his backs could run riot. Without the necessary platform laid down by the forward pack, Gale and the other playmakers would simply not have been as effective and Junior was one of the most crucial elements in getting Castleford on the front foot. The Samoan also possesses a nice offload which, after drawing in and often swatting away multiple defenders, enabled Castleford to penetrate further into the opposition's territory. This presence was evident against Leeds in March. Moors obtained the ball on his own 30-metre line and after rumbling past four defenders offloaded beautifully to Luke Gale who sidestepped the defence and kicked to Greg Minikin for a try of the season contender.

Junior also has a fantastic rugby brain taking the ball directly to the line then turning to pass, creating the essential space for his backs to exploit. With a fully fit and perfectly settled Junior Moors in 2018, the potential for him to rekindle his early 2017 form and perhaps go one better, is a scary thought.

@free_oakers84 – 10th August 2017: "Said it before and I'll say it again Junior is my favourite EVER Cas player with Dale Fritz a very close 2nd."

@MattCore180 – 25th July 2017: "@Jnrmoors the incredible hulk...throws other pros around like rag dolls and eats yards... be great to have you back out there in the 8s."

HOLMES THE HERO AS TIGERS DEFY THE ODDS

A depleted Castleford side were predicted to lose this fixture even before the team took to the field. But this was the Tigers of 2017 that we are talking about and the 17 men out on the gleaming Jungle pitch had the self-belief to inflict the first loss for Justin Holbrook since taking over as St Helens coach. After three games in ten days, Castleford were much-changed from the team that overcame the Leigh Centurions with ease. With England trio Zak Hardaker, Luke Gale and captain Michael Shenton, all out and with two debutants in the side, Jake Trueman and Kieran Gill, a strong Saints side were odds-on favourites to notch up a priceless victory. Tell that to Daryl Powell and his players; Full of vim and vigour, the Tigers were able to overcome a 12-4 deficit at half-time to stretch their unbeaten run to seven. The result was even more striking considering the Saints had had a nine-day rest. Mark Percival and Louie McCarthy-Scarsbrook crossed for the visitors in the first 40 minutes either side of a Kieran Gill try on debut, who had to hobble off not long after with a season-ending injury.

On a wet Sunday afternoon, chances were at a premium and it was imperative that the Tigers hit back first after the break. They did just that. Second-rower Mike McMeeken, in incredible form since his move from London in 2015 and not originally named in the team after England duty, blazed through a huge gap in the Saints defence to close the gap to just two points. The defence was essential and substitute Jy Hitchcox, playing his first game for Castleford since overcoming a career-threatening injury, made two try-saving tackles that had the Jungle in raptures.

As the second-half progressed, the tension became palpable. It was the Tigers who landed the killer blow when Greg Minikin put in a delightful grubber for the chasing

105

Tom Holmes to pounce and score. Saints tried desperately to reply but the Castleford defence held firm for what was a hard-earned victory. To win when it had seemed much easier to lose on paper was a sign of Daryl Powell's credentials as one of the best coaches in the game. A real motivator, but also an enforcer of rules and respect, the turnaround Castleford has witnessed since Powell took over has to be one of the greatest transformations in sporting history. This win against all odds was evidence of the effects that Powell has on the squad as a whole.

WHAT THE FANS SAID

@Martingrayston: "Biggest win of season that! #classycas #COYF."

@LeanneHirst: "Is this a dream? Cas 4 points clear at top of Super League."

@Castigers_JT: "And that's why we're classy Cas. What a performance from the young lads. Four points clear at the top of the league."

@grahamsmithctsc: "Absolutely outstanding performance from 1-17 @ CTRLFC still sitting proud on top of the league."

@tigerdeano: "Worst day ever to have hay fever…Best day ever to be a Cas fan #bittersweet."

KIERAN GILL SIGNS ONE-YEAR DEAL WITH THE CLUB HOLDING AN OPTION FOR A FURTHER TWO

Kieran, aged just 21, was a crucial figure in the Tigers Academy setup and was rewarded at 19 with a professional contract and he has been in and around the first-team set-up since. The former Lock Lane youngster was released from Castleford's scholarship in 2014 and made the move to Salford Red Devils only to return to the Tigers in 2015.

In 2016, he was sent on loan first to Oxford, then to Oldham Roughyeds where he played a key role in propelling Oldham to 6th in the Championship table. In 2017, he impressed further for Oldham, scoring five tries in nine games. He was then recalled for the St Helens match just three days prior to signing the new deal where he scored a try and generally looked comfortable in a much-changed team. Gill, unfortunately, suffered a season-ending injury in the first-half but carried on with a warrior-like determination as long as he could before he had to leave the field.

Kieran was jubilant to remain with his hometown club, a club he always supported as a boy: "It is a dream come true really, I took a long route in getting here but I've made sure that I believed in myself and I've worked hard to get to where I am. I've put a lot of hard work in and to be rewarded with a new contract is amazing and to be given a new deal for my hometown club, who I grew up supporting, is great. I must say thanks to all the coaching staff at Cas and also Oldham for helping me keep achieving and progressing as a young lad in this game. I wouldn't want to be anywhere else than Cas!

Kieran also enthused about the Tigers fans after his debut against St Helens just a few days before: "When I scored I couldn't believe that I had managed to get over on debut. I couldn't have dreamt of that happening but for it to happen at the Jungle where I was brought up in the crowd cheering the boys on was such an amazing feeling. To then walk back clapping the fans and them returning the applause was one of the best feelings ever. Hopefully, I can score many more tries as a Tigers player and I will look to cement myself around the first team with more appearances by doing what I love."

Powell stressed that Kieran had a big future at the club and backed him to overcome the injury that sidelined him for the rest of 2017: "Kieran Gill is a young player with loads of potential. He showed in his debut that he is a player with a really bright future ahead of him. He's tall and athletic with a great skill set, he can play in the centre and on the wing and I am delighted that he has agreed to sign. He's one of the next cabs off the rank and obviously it's disappointing he's got this injury but this gives him confidence that he can get back and get into our first team next year."

ALEX FOSTER SIGNS TWO-YEAR DEAL UNTIL END OF 2019

Alex had initially joined the club on trial way back in February and was granted an extension to his short contract. Despite a pectoral injury adding to his injury woes, Alex did enough, in Powell's eyes, to warrant a two-year contract. It must have been a weight off his shoulders given that at the start of the year he was without a club and suffering from injury. Having made his debut in the away win at Huddersfield in May, he improved with every game, becoming a fearsome defender with the ability to run fantastic attacking lines.

Alex was, of course, delighted to secure his once uncertain future: "I'm over the moon to sign here for another two years.

"It's a great place to be at the moment and everyone can see why with how well the boys are doing on the field.

"I'm really happy to be working with this group of players and the staff as well and I can't wait for the next two years."

Powell was enthusiastic about Alex's potential role in the team, with Alex having overcome a less than satisfactory pre-season and injuries to impress Powell in his short time at the club: "I've been really impressed with Alex since he arrived at the club.

"He hasn't had a pre-season and he's had minimal game time, but he's battled his way through all of that and a couple of injuries and he looks like he's going to be a really strong player for us.

"The games in which he has played, he has been tough and aggressive. He's got some work to do on his skill sets and understanding our game, but his defensive mentality is absolutely superb and some of his line running is great and he's only going to get better within our environment."

Alex definitely continued to get better within the Castleford environment and became one of the Tigers' most consistent and ever-present players by the end of the season. It was a remarkable turnaround for someone who could well have drifted out of the game in February.

ANDY LYNCH TO RETIRE AT THE END OF 2017 SEASON

Andy is a stalwart of the game and will make history as one of only two players, the other being Kevin Sinfield, to register 500 career appearances. This is no mean feat for a prop forward who was always leading from the front and putting his body on the line.

For Andy, therefore, he will see out his career at the club where his illustrious career began. Lynch made his professional debut back in 1999 with the Tigers as a 19-year old after coming through the Castleford academy ranks.

While with the Tigers, Lynch represented Yorkshire and England whilst also being selected in the 2003 Super League Dream Team. Andy went on to earn five England caps and one for Great Britain.

Following Castleford's painful relegation in 2004, Lynch headed to Bradford Bulls where he spent six years. He was a key figure in the Bulls' Grand Final winning campaign in 2005 as well as in the World Club Challenge in 2006, where Bradford comfortably beat Wests Tigers 30-10. His 2006 season with the Bulls became one of his best in his career, earning a call-up to the Great Britain squad for the 2006 Tri-Nations tournament. However, to his frustration, he did not register an appearance in any games. Lynch received his one and only Great Britain cap the following year when he played in a test match against France. Injuries in 2008, however, ruled Andy out of England's Rugby League World Cup squad when he looked destined to be a crucial figure.

In 2011, Lynch was on the move, this time to Hull FC for a significant six-figure sum after six years at Bradford. Andy signed a two-year deal. For the 2012 season, he had the honour of being named captain, so large was the respect he commanded.

Andy became the prodigal son when he returned to the Tigers aged 33 in 2014, signing an initial two-year deal. But due to his continued good form, Andy earned an extended contract to take him into 2017.

Andy obviously felt the time was right to go, not just for his body, but to watch his children grow up and commit more to his family: "I discussed it a lot with my wife April and we decided it's the right time for me now to look to the next chapter of my life. My three boys are at that age now where I need to be there more at the weekend, they are all playing sports and I've already missed out on a lot with them. It's now time to turn the tables and for me to spend my weekend watching my boys play sports."

Powell was keen to underline Andy's impact on the Tigers but also the game as a whole and his legendary status within the sport: "Andy has been a great servant to both Castleford Tigers and Rugby League. He epitomises the word professional! We have all enjoyed many hours watching him play the game he clearly loves, and we all wish him well for the rest of this season and for the next chapter of his career."

#18 - Matt Cook

Date of Birth: 14/11/1986
Height: 183cm (6 ft)
Weight: 105kg (16.5 stone)
Country: England
Position: Prop/Second-Row
Previous Clubs: Bradford Bulls, Hull KR, London Broncos
National Honours: 2 caps for England

Appearances: 22	**Avg. Gain:** 7.53
Tries: 3	**Tackles:** 459
Try Assists: 0	**Clean Breaks:** 0
Metres: 1672	**Offloads:** 3

Matt joined the club ahead of the 2015 season from London Broncos after their turbulent last season in Super League. He was a force to be reckoned with from the start of his Tigers career.

Matt runs straight at his opponents which enables him to make substantial yardage whilst carrying two or three defenders with him. In his time with the Tigers, Matt has developed from a back-rower into more of a hard-hitting front-rower and took his strength and explosive power to a new level, punching holes in rival defensive lines.

Tragedy struck though at the end of May when Matt was the recipient of a dangerous 'cannonball' tackle in the away drubbing of Leigh and subsequently missed seven games. Cook made his return in the victory at Catalans in July and, not forgetting the fact that this was his first game in two months, he went hammer and tong with the massive Dragons pack. Cook would make only two more appearances until he was again sidelined, this time with a back problem. And unfortunately for Matt, he missed the historic League Leaders' Shield game against Wakefield in August.

Once again though, Matt bounced back, missing only three games and playing a key role in Castleford's against-the-odds victory at Wigan in mid-September as well as showing up well in the Grand Final defeat at Old Trafford. Cook's herculean efforts on the pitch in 2017, particularly in his comeback games following injuries is a testament to another fantastic buy by Daryl Powell.

Matt's form has gone up level after level and 2017 can surely be recognised as his best in a Tigers shirt. Injury-free, Matt is one of the most consistent forwards in the Tigers' pack and all being well, he can demonstrate this regularly in 2018.

@MarkRammond – 9th October 2017: "You were the only forward in a Cas shirt who held the ball and made metres Cookie. But you couldn't win it on your own. Gutted for you mate."

@cwalker_1995 – 10th October 2017: "Just watched the Grand Final again and how good was Matt Cook?! Must be the most underrated forward in Super League #somanymetres."

@bigladmd – 18th August 2017: "You have played a massive part of this success, be very proud."

EDEN SCORES FIVE AS THE TIGERS PUNISH THE WOLVES

In the weeks prior to this home game, bar the St Helens match where he played at full-back, Greg Eden's try-scoring exploits had become something of a routine. This 36-16 victory was yet another example of an Eden masterclass; five tries pulled him level in the Castleford history books for the most in a game and up to 30 for the season thus far. Warrington, on the other hand, produced yet another dismal performance fraught with indiscipline to take their losing run to five. Both Chris Hill and Tom Lineham were sin-binned, the former as early as the seventh minute for a late tackle on Luke Gale. Greg Eden had already scored once in the second minute after he did splendidly to take a towering Gale kick, and in Hill's absence, Eden got his second following a great move down the blindside. The impressive Mike McMeeken fed Greg Minikin with a superb flick pass in the 11th minute and the former then scored himself courtesy of a Gale pass after a brilliant Nathan Massey drive.

By the time Hill returned, the visitors were 22-0 down. Four tries in just 15 minutes had left the visitors shell-shocked and with the game already seemingly out of reach, the Wolves recorded their first points through a Tom Lineham try. But another Eden try in the 28th minute took the hosts into the dressing rooms with a 26-6 lead. In what was veteran prop Andy Lynch's 500th career appearance, the Tigers continued their onslaught after the break as Eden racked up another two scores in the first quarter of the second-half. His first followed a trademark lightning-quick break from Ben Roberts and his second came after fast hands from Gale, Zak Hardaker and Michael Shenton. As Castleford took their foot off the gas, ex-Tiger

Joe Westerman did cross in the 52nd minute and Jack Hughes in the 72nd minute to give the scoreline some respectability, but the afternoon once again belonged to Eden and the Tigers.

The victory was however marred by a severe-looking knee injury to barnstorming forward Junior Moors who was later confirmed to be out for approximately eight weeks. The Samoan had been in inspired form for the West Yorkshire club and would be a huge gap to fill, especially as the Challenge Cup quarter-final against Hull FC beckoned. A pleasing victory nonetheless as the Tigers moved six points clear at the top of the table.

WHAT THE FANS SAID

@Nevchenko5: "Scrappy 2nd half but seriously, what a time to be a Cas fan! 6 pts clear and Cup QF next week. Hope Moors is ok. #COYF #daretodream."

@jamiedunnell10: "Credit to @GregEden1 top finisher but gotta credit @mshenton22 @snozzer_gale and everyone else for the passes and plays for him to score."

@aliicebro: "Six points clear at the top, happy birthday me."

@PhilDransfield: "Another enjoyable afternoon watching the mighty @CTRLFC win, it's better than the early 90's, we were good then, but this is another level."

@saralclose: "Brilliant win to celebrate @8AndyLynch's 500th game. 500!!! What an achievement."

BLACK AND WHITES TOO STRONG AS TIGERS CRASH OUT OF THE CUP

Whilst in the league, the Tigers could do no wrong, the Challenge Cup saw a Castleford defeat for the first time in nine games. The loss of Junior Moors in the previous week's victory over Warrington was a big one, even more so when considering the size of the Hull FC forward pack and their two wingers, Fetuli Talanoa and Mahe Fonua.

The match could not have started much worse for the Tigers as in the fourth minute Carlos Tuimavave intercepted a pass from half-back Ben Roberts to go the length of the field after the visitors looked like scoring themselves. Fetuli Talanoa then powered his way over Greg Minikin in the corner eight minutes later to double the hosts' lead. Castleford finally replied when Ben Roberts picked up a loose ball and sped through some soft defence to register a much-needed Castleford try with 13 minutes to go until half-time.

This try kicked the visitors into life and after upping the ante, the momentum swung the Tigers' way when a fine reverse kick by Luke Gale saw Zak Hardaker touch down beside the posts just three minutes after Roberts' effort. With Gale converting both, the scores were locked at 12 apiece. The final score of the half went to the home side as referee Phil Bentham awarded Hull a penalty which Jake Connor duly converted to give Hull a 14-12 half-time lead. Although Roberts crossed for his second seven minutes after the restart, which gave Castleford a slender lead, Connor kicked three more penalties in the second-half. Hull then pulled away in the 65th minute, buoyed by the huge metres they were making in midfield when Mahe Fonua and Jamie Shaul scored within three minutes of each other to take the game away from the visitors.

Greg Minikin's late try with eight minutes remaining, after an off-the-cuff last tackle move, set up a tense finish but Hull's defence stood strong to propel them into the semi-finals and another step towards defending the Challenge Cup. The Tigers, on the other hand, would see this defeat as a missed opportunity to knock out the holders.

The only positive that could be taken from this devastating loss was the fact that later down the line it gave the Tigers two valuable two-week rests at the end of July and mid-August that allowed key players vital recuperation for the Grand Final charge.

WHAT THE FANS SAID

@emmarshy: "Hull out muscled us, limited time in their half and our play has looked desperate at times. Well deserved winners #CCHulCas."

@jonny_binns: "As much as I hate losing it could be a blessing in disguise. Get a couple of weeks off at the business end of the season could do us a favour."

@BizarreRl: "What frustrates me is that we had the game at 16-18, then just lost our heads. Not champion mentality; but as with all season, we'll learn."

RossWilliams_: "Gutted, but all speed ahead to the league leaders' shield now. Looking forward to a big response at Headingley."

@JoshCheetham91: "Our own worst enemies here. Nobody to blame but ourselves."

#19 - Gadwin Springer

Date of Birth: 04/04/1993
Height: 191cm (6 ft 3)
Weight: 113kg (17.8 stone)
Country: France
Position: Prop
Previous Clubs: Catalans Dragons
National Honours: 5 caps for France

Appearances: 21	**Avg. Gain:** 7.09
Tries: 1	**Tackles:** 291
Try Assists: 1	**Clean Breaks:** 1
Metres: 1077	**Offloads:** 5

Gadwin joined the club midway through the 2015 season on a two-and-a-half-year deal from Catalans for whom he made just four appearances. With raw skills and an inability to speak fluent English, it took time for Gadwin to settle in West Yorkshire. The 2016 season, however, saw him become a monster in the Castleford pack, notching up 21 appearances and scoring three tries. The impression Springer had created was rewarded with an improved two-year deal in February 2017 to take his contract to the end of 2019.

Castleford fans were expecting, after his tremendous showing in 2016 that in 2017, Gadwin to kick on and become a real force to be reckoned with in Super League. However, he was used only sporadically by Powell. When he did come on, Gadwin still had something about him; his sheer power and enthusiastic running was a welcome sight to the Tigers faithful and the crowd repeatedly rose when Gadwin charged the ball into the opposition's line. In May, a rampaging 20-metre run through the heart of the Widnes defence for a brilliant individual effort that only Gadwin could score had the Jungle's spectators on their feet and was scored at a crucial time when the Tigers were up against it. 2017, whilst it was perhaps not the best of years for Gadwin in terms of game time and consistency, was a necessary stepping stone for the prop forward to develop his game. One must also take into consideration that Gadwin turned only 24 in April 2017.

Whilst 2017 didn't see him feature as much as he would have wanted, Gadwin still made the France squad for the World Cup in 2017 and will be looking to push on further in 2018.

@WidnesRL – 26th May 2017: "39' Try to the hosts, as Gadwin Springer charges through the middle and slams the ball down next to the posts – 8-12."
@CTRLFC – 19th March 2017: "52: Matt Cook comes off with Gadwin Springer coming on to the chants of 'Jerry Jerry' from the crowd."
@James27LUFC – 10th February 2017: "Love me some Gadwin Springer! #COYF."

RUTHLESS TIGERS BEAT TOOTHLESS RHINOS

Following Castleford's exit from the Challenge Cup, the Tigers were searching for a reply and to extend their six-point gap at the top of the table to seven. Questioned by much of the Rugby League fraternity on their ability to win big games following last week's Cup defeat at the hands of Hull FC, the Tigers responded in the best way possible. The game was finely poised come half-time at just 8-6 to the visitors. A bizarre converted Ash Handley try after Ben Roberts had attempted a ridiculous pass behind his own line had given the Rhinos the lead in the eighth minute. Then controversially, Greg Eden touched down in the corner on 14 minutes after referee Robert Hicks ruled Paul McShane had been stripped of the ball when it appeared he'd simply lost the ball. A Luke Gale penalty seven minutes from the end of the half gave the visitors the advantage, but more controversy descended upon Headingley and referee Hicks as Leeds believed they had scored after the hooter had sounded only for Hicks to be already travelling towards the tunnel for half-time.

Castleford, under the cosh both on the field and from the stands, turned the screw in the second-half. Tigers fullback Zak Hardaker, in his first game back at Headingley following his controversial season-long loan to the Tigers, which was made into a permanent four-and-a-half year deal just four days after this victory, silenced the Rhinos' vociferous crowd with a brilliant long-range effort on 45 minutes after shrugging off the attention of covering fullback Liam Sutcliffe. A remarkable play on the last tackle then saw Grant Millington score seven minutes later. His intelligent thinking to point to where he wanted Gale to kick showcased his class. This try put clear daylight between the two sides for the first time as Castleford led 6-20.

And although Leeds hit back through prop Adam Cuthbertson in the 60th minute, the

hosts could find no momentum to avoid an astonishing seventh loss in a row against the Tigers. The icing on the cake proved to be Gale's drop-goal in the dying stages, a cheeky way for the Tigers to finish the game and chalk up a seventh successive win over the Rhinos.

Following the misery of the Cup exit, Castleford bounced back remarkably well to stretch their unbeaten run in the league to nine and extend their lead at the top of the table to seven points. Next week would be payback time as Hull FC, twice victors over the Tigers in 2017, rolled into the Mend-a-Hose Jungle for a colossal encounter.

WHAT THE FANS SAID

@LeanneHirst: "After watching us lose to Leeds by 70 plus points for years, I'll never bore of us beating them!! I chuffing love you Cas Tigers."

@chapperz1973: "Outstanding performance from my beloved @ CTRLFC tonight. Title winning form. Amazing how Daryl Powell has turned us round."

@expressbrandbiz: "Thought it was so nice how we gave Leeds a couple of tries to make them feel involved a bit."

@LaurenciumSmith: "Massive win for the tigers tonight!!!! Hard fought, well deserved!!! 7/7 #COYF @ CTRLFC #CastlefordTigers #SweetCaroline."

@ClarksonSte: "7 in a row #COYF."

ZAK HARDAKER MAKES HIS MOVE TO THE TIGERS PERMANENT ON A FOUR-AND-A-HALF-YEAR DEAL

Zak had initially been on loan at the Tigers from the start of the season but so good were his performances and his attitude, that the decision to sign him permanently was done in June, rather than in November as was first intended.

Any Castleford fan could see how eager Zak had been to find his feet under the tutelage of Powell, who had overseen his development at Featherstone and handed him his professional debut as an 18-year old. The 2017 season really saw Zak's form of 2015 return. He fit like a glove into the fullback role and was a crucial asset in Castleford's triumphant year. Indeed just four days before this news was announced, Zak had scored a spectacular long-range effort against his old club at Headingley much to the joy of the travelling Castleford fans.

Zak was understandably ecstatic to finally sort out his future after an uncertain few months: "I am really thankful for the opportunity that Daryl Powell and Steve Gill gave me to come to Castleford at the start of the season. To get the chance to stay here, I just jumped at the offer! I have fully enjoyed my time here so far and I think we have a couple of exciting years ahead of us. It was an easy decision to stay here once I got the offer."

Hardaker added: "The fans are amazing! It's quite a close-knit community and the fans are so loyal. It's great for myself to be around the club and I really enjoy playing for the people of Cas."

Zak clearly felt at home in 2017 with his performances on the field reflecting that. He obviously enjoyed playing for his new club and their followers.

Powell reckoned Zak's signature showed how far Castleford had come. The club could now attract world-class, international-standard players: "Signing Zak is a huge deal for the club. For quality players and indeed international players to come to Castleford and then want to stay and commit their long-term futures here, I feel says a lot about us as a club.

"Zak is continuing to improve as a player and I believe he will continue to do so over the coming seasons. I look forward to working with Zak and helping him firstly to do something special with Castleford and then grow as an international player and play in the World Cup at the end of the season."

DANIEL IGBINEDION SIGNS FOR FEATHERSTONE ROVERS UNTIL END OF THE SEASON AFTER RELEASE

Daniel had signed with the Tigers before the season started, looking to force his way into the first-team squad. However, with him competing for such hotly-contested positions (front and back row) and on the back of such a successful year for the Tigers, chances were at a premium for Daniel which meant he played the vast majority of 2017 at Dewsbury Rams. Castleford released him from his contract so he could join Featherstone Rovers until the end of 2017.

On his departure, Daniel thanked the club for giving him the opportunity in a full-time environment to grow as a player and a person, but he acknowledged the fact that the time was right for him to play consistently at a competitive level: "I've really enjoyed my time here at Castleford Tigers, and I'm really grateful to Daryl Powell and Steve Gill for allowing me to come here and train in a professional full-time environment. I've learnt so much here but ultimately my goal is to be playing Rugby League week in week out. I'm excited about the fresh start at Featherstone Rovers and I'm looking forward to getting stuck into training this week with my new teammates."

Powell thanked him for his hard work and understood that a move to Featherstone was the best way forward for Daniel: "Dan worked hard during his time at Castleford without being able to break into the first team. An opportunity to play regularly in the Championship became available and Featherstone will offer him a great chance to develop further and I wish him all the best for the future."

#20 - Larne Patrick

Date of Birth: 03/11/1988
Height: 183cm (6 ft)
Weight: 108kg (17 stone)
Country: Wales
Position: Prop
Previous Clubs: Huddersfield Giants,
Wigan Warriors (loan)
National Honours: 3 caps for Wales

Appearances: 6	**Avg. Gain:** 8.05
Tries: 0	**Tackles:** 96
Try Assists: 0	**Clean Breaks:** 0
Metres: 330	**Offloads:** 1

Larne joined the Tigers midway through the 2016 season on an initial loan from Huddersfield Giants. He went on to secure a three-year deal at the end of 2016 that would keep him at Castleford until 2019.

Unfortunately for Larne, he did not reach the heights that first attracted Powell to his signature, and instead missed long periods of the season through injury. The back end of 2016 and 2017 was a tough ride for Patrick; he should have been back playing at the beginning of the 2017 season, but his first wrist operation failed. The second thankfully was successful but he was now far behind his recovery schedule. A traumatic and nightmarish nine-month absence from the field meant Larne would only make his first appearance of the season in the Challenge Cup defeat at Hull in June. He would make just three more appearances after the Hull game before he was again sidelined with niggling issues. Larne would go on to play in three Super 8s games (St Helens, Huddersfield, and Leeds), but failed to earn a spot in the semi-final or the Grand Final.

Larne is a blockbuster of a player and his yardage was impressive in the small cameos he managed during 2017. Against his old side Huddersfield in September, he notched up a quite remarkable average carry gain of 9.8 metres, the highest in the team. Larne's aggressive and direct running was a great sight to see when he was in a Castleford shirt and he was certainly not afraid to get stuck in while defending. His determination to recover from his lengthy time out of the team and what could have been a career-threatening problem was unwavering, as was his desire to play for the Castleford badge. On the field, Larne's hard-hitting capabilities and no-nonsense style of play earned him a plethora of admirers from the Tigers fans.

In October 2017, it was confirmed Castleford had released him by mutual consent, and Larne moved to Leigh Centurions on a two-year deal.

@MattCore180 – 25th July 2017: "@LPatrick_18 such a shame injury has dogged you this year because the performances you have turned in have been mighty...stick at it mate."

@stoner85 – 24th June 2017: "@LPatrick_18 what a performance big man...was like watching a bull charge round the pitch...bet a few rhinos had you in nightmares last night."

TIGERS FINALLY END HULL HOODOO

Hull FC, the only team to have beaten the Tigers twice this season, came to the Mend-a-Hose Jungle knowing that they had so far had the measure of the Tigers. Yet revenge was sweet for the Tigers as they produced a dominant display that saw them 22-4 up at one stage.

The visitors did, however, strike first as a remarkable Jake Connor offload somehow found Mahe Fonua who touched down for the first points of the night in the sixth minute. Castleford were brought back into the game by the Airlie Birds themselves as a wayward pass by ex-Tiger Marc Sneyd was gobbled up by the outstanding scrum-half Luke Gale who dotted down for an opportunist try. Now the Tigers took control, but they also had the visitors to thank for their next points as Fetuli Talanoa fumbled a high Gale kick which provided a gift for second-rower Mike McMeeken on 22 minutes.

Stern Castleford defence, in which they kept the visitors out despite five consecutive sets on their own line, showed the improvements that coach Daryl Powell had been calling for since their Challenge Cup exit. Yet another Hull mistake then allowed the Tigers to extend their lead further as Zak Hardaker grabbed a wonderful solo try after Hull full-back Jamie Shaul had attempted a chip over the Tigers' defence practically on the hooter. These converted tries, as well as a Gale penalty, had established a 20-4 lead for the hosts and another Gale penalty early in the second-half extended this lead by another two.

The match descended into somewhat of a stalemate until the visitors produced a near-remarkable comeback. Sika Manu was harshly denied a try for a knock-on before Fonua grabbed his second with 15 minutes to go. Gale then soon re-established a three-try lead with another penalty in

the 70th minute before Talanoa crossed twice to ensure a nervy finish. Hull took the match all the way to the hooter and only a forward pass when the siren had already gone stopped them in their tracks. Another invaluable two points for the Tigers opened up a seemingly unassailable eight-point lead at the top of the table and demonstrated that the Hull forward pack, which had dominated Cas twice already, could be stopped.

It was vital that the Tigers' mental block against the Airlie Birds be eradicated before the business end of the season. Despite the late scare, Powell would have been ecstatic with the way his players had been in complete control for most of the game. He would also have been pleased to know that the Tigers would finish top at the end of the regular season.

WHAT THE FANS SAID

@HantsCastiger: "I've followed @ CTRLFC for 37 years and never been so proud."

@HelsG12: "Just watched Friday's game back and @ Massey196 you put in one hell of a shift lad!! One of the most underrated players going."

@stephyhull: "WE ARE TOP OF THE LEEEEEAGUE."

@AFenton90: "Tonight is the first time this season (20 games) that the opposition has scored more tries than us. @CTRLFC."

@LaurenciumSmith: "Massive win for the tigers tonight @zakhardaker1 had a stormer! What a game! #COYF #CastlefordTigers #SLCasHul."

123

JOYOUS JULY

MIKE McMEEKEN SIGNS TWO-YEAR CONTRACT EXTENSION UNTIL THE END OF 2020

Mike joined the Tigers from London Broncos at the end of the 2014 season on a two-year deal. Mike was one of the stars that shone during a painful relegation season for the Broncos and Powell saw his potential. Mike surprised everybody with the way he developed in 2015 and was an ever-present towards the back end of the year, making 17 consecutive appearances and scoring two tries.

His performances impressed so much that he was rewarded with another two-year deal in November 2015. His year-by-year ability just kept on growing and by 2017, he was widely tipped for England honours. His fine form throughout the season duly earned him a place in Wayne Bennett's England Elite Performance Squad, making his debut v Samoa in the Pacific Test in May where he went well. Still only 23, Mike has the potential to be an absolute world-beater in the future.

McMeeken, upon signing his extension, could not praise the coaching staff enough for his development as a player: "It was a straightforward decision to stay here. Since I've joined the club, I've loved my time here. The club came to me with an offer and it was a pretty simple decision for me to stay,"

McMeeken added: "I was half the player I was when I joined this club. I knew I had the ability, but being around Powelly (Daryl Powell) and the rest of the coaches has helped me develop as a player."

Powell lauded Mike's improvements since he came to the club and rightly spoke of his key role at the club as well as his international future in the game: "It is fantastic news for the club that Mike has agreed to extend his contract. We have a strong desire to keep our best players at the club and build on the journey that we have started by developing individual players and our squad moving forward. Mike has developed into one of the best back-rowers in the country and we think there is further development in his game over the coming seasons. I look forward to working with Mike on improving his game and hopefully seeing him do special things with the Tigers and in the World Cup for England at the end of the season."

#21 - Joel Monaghan

Date of Birth: 22/04/1982
Height: 187cm (6 ft 1)
Weight: 99kg (15.6 stone)
Country: Australia
Position: Wing
Previous Clubs: Canberra Raiders, Sydney Roosters, Warrington Wolves
National Honours: 5 caps for Australia

Appearances: 17	**Avg. Gain:** 7.82
Tries: 8	**Tackles:** 42
Try Assists: 1	**Clean Breaks:** 11
Metres: 985	**Offloads:** 4

Joel came to the club ahead of the 2016 season having enjoyed four successful years at Warrington where he won a Challenge Cup medal and the League Leaders' Shield. Joel also represented New South Wales twice in State of Origin. Monaghan made 18 appearances in his first year at the club, scoring 18 tries.

He saw his chances in the first-team limited in 2017 but he still managed to register an impressive eight tries in 17 games. His ability to leap graciously in the air meant that Joel was a perfect target for an attacking kick, but it also ensured that he was capable of defusing an opponent's kick to the corner with relative ease. This trademark of his was on show in the nailbiting victory away at Huddersfield in May when Paul McShane directed a towering kick for Joel to claim. Joel plucked the ball out of the air despite the attentions of the Huddersfield defence and calmly offloaded to Greg Eden who dotted down over the whitewash for a fine try.

2017 was also confirmed to be Monaghan's last season at the Tigers, and whilst some fans were questioning the decision to bring him to the club at the age of 33, almost all have recognised the contribution that Joel has made to the club. His experience and knowledge of his position and the game have been crucial in the development of players such as Greg Minikin. Joel was also a vital squad player for Castleford in 2017, filling in for injuries in the backline. It was expected that Joel would leave the club at the end of 2017 after his contract ran out which Daryl Powell confirmed at the clubs' awards dinner. But Castleford fans must salute one of the greats of the game and a player who has been essential in driving the standards and the culture of the club that made 2017 possible.

@MichaelBrannan – 7th October 2017: "Think Cas made an error not picking Joel Monaghan. Experience matters in these games."

@M_Shaw1 – 3rd August 2017: "That is an absolutely outstanding finish from Joel Monaghan. Not bad for a 35-year-old!"

@nathastbury – 6th April 2017: "Thought Joel Monaghan was superb at short notice too and a great sign of his integrity that he didn't want to be subbed off."

GALE WINS THE DAY WITH LAST-MINUTE DROP-GOAL

After two bruising encounters against their closest rivals in the Super League table, Castleford went into this local derby full of confidence and expectation. Yet Trinity had other ideas. A quite unbelievable 16-0 half-time deficit left Castleford fans scratching their heads as to what had gone wrong in the first-half.

It is obvious the impact that Trinity's head of rugby, John Kear has had on the Wakefield club and before the game, he roused the Trinity players to give his old club "a good hiding". The Tigers simply could not live with the opposition's onslaught which was epitomised by Wakefield coach Chris Chester's inclusion of four front-row forwards on the bench. The Tigers did, however, gift Trinity their first score. Jesse Sene-Lefao's careless offload was snapped up by second rower Dean Hadley and a neat pass to winger Ben Jones-Bishop saw the pacey winger outstrip the Castleford defence and race 80 metres for his 17th Super League try of the season. That ninth-minute try converted by Finn stunned the Tigers and four successive penalties enabled Wakefield to pile on the pressure with Finn extending the lead with the first of two penalties. Then, ten minutes before half-time, hooker Kyle Wood wriggled over for another Trinity score after fullback Scott Grix had been held up just short. Another Finn penalty meant the hosts were up 16-0 as the teams left the field for half-time.

80 minutes had passed since the Tigers last registered a try following their scoreless second-half against Hull FC and the first-half against Trinity. But the Castleford supporters did not have long to wait. Two tries in the first five minutes enabled the Tigers to reduce the arrears. Winger Greg Eden sprinted 90 metres after pouncing on a handling error by former Tiger Joe Arundel and then prop Grant Millington took a short ball from Paul McShane to crash over next to the posts. With Gale successful with both conversions, the Tigers were only four points behind. They took the lead when Greg

128

Minikin fed the powerful Mike McMeeken in the 54th minute which Gale converted.

The home side, shellshocked, would not lie down, regardless of the Tigers' increased intensity and Trinity looked to have won it when David Fifita, only named in the team a few minutes before kick-off, barged over the line with 11 minutes left. With a Finn conversion and penalty, the hosts were up 24-18.

Almost immediately, the Tigers responded as centre Jake Webster showed tremendous power to score a converted try. And then, hero-turned-villain, David Fifita gave the Tigers good field position with an unnecessary penalty from the resulting kick-off from which Luke Gale slotted over a one-pointer with a minute to go.

It was a lucky escape for the Tigers but their seventh victory in a row against Trinity had enabled them to establish a massive ten-point gap at the top of the table. This undoubtedly left the Tigers with one hand on the League Leaders' Shield.

WHAT THE FANS SAID

@underwood_81: "Sign of a decent team is to play that badly and still find a win. Wakey stuck it to us though, we need to learn from this game. #COYF."

@Garethvicar: "Phew that was a get out of jail free card tonight."

@RossWilliams_: "Don't know how we won that. Don't care. Talk about a game of two halves. #COYF."

@therealBennoooo: "Some say that the best teams have to win ugly…we saw the worst 40 mins of the season, not sure it was undeserved tho #coyf."

@TigersFaithful: "How the hell did we win that? Completely undeserved, but we have found a way to win once again."

#22 - Will Maher

Date of Birth: 04/11/1995
Height: 196cm (6 ft 4)
Weight: 113kg (17.8 stone)
Country: England
Position: Prop
Previous Clubs: Oxford RLFC (loan),
Batley Bulldogs (loan)

Appearances: 1	**Avg. Gain:** 6.14
Tries: 0	**Tackles:** 16
Try Assists: 0	**Clean Breaks:** 0
Metres: 43	**Offloads:** 0

Will has a background unlike any other at the club: he was the first player to graduate from the RFL Regional Academy programme and sign a professional contract. Will initially joined the Tigers on a 12-month loan from the Cumbrian Academy in September 2013, but he made a quick and lasting impression earning a professional deal by December that year.

Will made his debut for the Tigers away at Warrington Wolves in 2014 aged just 18. Maher transformed into a more consistent part of Powell's squad in 2015 and 2016 notching up 15 appearances in the latter. With a big future ahead of him, Will was rewarded for his hard work and determination with a four-year extension signed in 2015 that will see the Cumbrian at the club until at least 2019.

In 2017, Will only registered one appearance with the Tigers against Hull FC in Castleford's last Super 8s home game, he was also named on the bench against Leeds in March but was an unused substitute. He played a pivotal role for Batley Bulldogs who finished sixth in the Championship and were semi-finalists in the Championship shield (although he missed the semi-final because of his inclusion in the Tigers' team to face Hull). Known for his huge frame, 'Big Will', as he is aptly nicknamed, proved to be a big favourite amongst the Batley spectators, taking in massive drives and attracting multiple defenders as well as sporting an enthusiastic and determined attitude in defence. On the field for around 30 minutes in his only game for the Tigers in September, Will looked comfortable at the top level. Although Will appeared to struggle with the intensity at times, he did make some good drives and several big tackles defence.

The future for Will, like himself, looks huge with Will having all the attributes to be a potential key player for the Tigers in the future.

@BatleyRLFC - 12th March 2017: "18' Batley are making plenty of metres through the middle through the big men, @ OfficialBullsRL defence is struggling with Will Maher."
@Bulldogs_Daily - 9th April 2017: "BOOM BOOM BOOM, SHAKE THE ROOM!! TRY!!!! Will Maher doesn't mess about and is over under the sticks."

SALFORD SHOWN NO MERCY BY THE DEVILISH TIGERS

After three close and gruelling tests for the Tigers in recent weeks, Salford rocked up to the Jungle having lost four in their last five games.

And, the visitors' loss in confidence was clear as early as the third minute when Greg Eden scored his 36th try of the campaign following a cut-out pass by Luke Gale. The Red Devils responded in perfect fashion after Greg Eden, known for his 'rocks and diamonds' characteristics, spilt the ball deep inside the Tigers' own half which gave the visitors good field position. Gareth O'Brien duly exploited it by dummying his way over in the eighth minute. A fantastic Paul McShane 40/20 midway through the first-half took the momentum back the Tigers' way as Ben Roberts powered over in the resulting set. Another Eden try three minutes later appeared to take the game away from the visitors, but the winger was clearly in agony after his masterful finish and had to be helped from the field and the stadium with a sling over his shoulder, a dislocated shoulder being the prognosis. Gale's second successive conversion put the hosts 16-4 up and the half-back then extended this by two with a penalty in the 32nd minute.

Salford did, however, keep themselves in the game with a Kris Welham effort seven minutes before half-time after a great break from standout Devils player Robert Lui. Down only 18-10 at the break, the Red Devils found themselves 24-10 down seven minutes after the restart as Castleford worked the short side well and Joel Monaghan, brought on in place of the injured Eden, dotted down. Four minutes later and the Tigers were in again, this time courtesy of Zak Hardaker following a terrific break from Michael Shenton. A Jake Bibby try for the visitors near the hour mark reduced the deficit to 16.

But all hope was ended when Monaghan scored his second in the 64th minute after yet another assist by his centre Shenton. A miserable evening for Salford was complete

when former Tigers forward Weller Hauraki was sin-binned for a late tackle on Grant Millington.

A competent performance for the Tigers was however greatly marred by the discomfort Eden was in as he left the field. Luckily for Castleford, the injury would not be as bad as first feared and he would be missing for only three games. The Red Devils were no match for a Castleford outfit who had now registered an astonishing 11 league wins in a row.

WHAT THE FANS SAID

@Jules_1961: "Well done @CTRLFC #WeAreTopOfTheLeague a say #WeAreTopOfTheLeague. Absolutely gutted for Eden, sending well wishes."

@LeanneHirst: "Remember when we couldn't win a game, now we've beaten every team at least once this season."

@jodi_1991: "Unbeaten at home in the regular season and 8 points clear at the top. You beauties. Can you imagine believing 4/5 years ago that we'd top of the league? It wasn't even a pipe dream for me. I just wanted to make top 8."

@lizfox67: "@GregEden1 gutted for you. Hope everything works out OK and you're not out too long #speedyrecovery."

@LadyWessie: "Love Jesse! He's literally the happiest guy ever! Loves Cas and is proud to wear the shirt…The world needs more Jesses!"

#23 - Tom Holmes

Date of Birth: 02/03/1996
Height: 177cm (5 ft 8)
Weight: 85kg (13.4 stone)
Country: England
Position: Scrum-half
Previous Clubs: Oxford RLFC (loan),
Batley Bulldogs (loan)

Appearances: 12	**Avg. Gain:** 8.95
Tries: 2	**Tackles:** 98
Try Assists: 0	**Clean Breaks:** 2
Metres: 179	**Offloads:** 1

Having come through the ranks at Castleford as a 14-year old, Tom went on to captain the Academy team before making the step up to the first-team squad. Tom debuted for the Tigers back in 2015 and made seven appearances during the 2016 season.

Behind Ben Roberts and Luke Gale in the Castleford half-back pecking order, Tom spent a period of 2017 on loan at Batley scoring three tries in eight games. Yet when called upon by Powell, he always delivered whether at scrum-half or at hooker (as he played in the away win at Wigan in September). Despite only being 21, Tom showed maturity when entrusted by Powell to direct the team and was not afraid to bark the orders at his much older teammates. Tom's most unforgettable moment in 2017 has to be his try at the Magic Weekend in May against the Tigers' bitter rivals Leeds. A poor kick by Danny McGuire landed straight into Holmes' grateful arms and he had the pace to run 90 metres and celebrate in front of the Castleford fans behind the sticks. As a Castleford fan, there was no better feeling for Tom than to touch down just below the celebrating fans. Tom's passion for the club is undeniable and the spirit, energy and humility he expressed when wearing the Castleford jersey was unparalleled.

Although Tom was under contract for 2018, he was keen to experience regular first-team rugby. A deal signed with Featherstone Rovers means that Tom will ply his trade in the Championship next season despite the attention of a Super League club and playing a good role in Castleford's record-breaking season.

Tom leaves with both the thanks and goodwill of all Castleford fans, and hopefully, as he stated in his parting interview, Tom will in the future return to his boyhood club.

@spriceldpuk - 10th September 2017: "Sorry to see you go, class act with a bright future, you've played your part in a historic year for our club, all the best Tom."

@stoner85 - 22nd May 2017: "Man of match amongst men of steel yesterday pal...really stepped up to plate and proved you can cut it amongst the best #COYF."

@Becky_Wuu – 21st May 2017: "Tom Holmes is 21 scoring tries like that and I'm 22, slightly hungover and about to inhale copious amounts of fried chicken. #COYF."

11 MEN? NO PROBLEM: TIGERS REGISTER ASTONISHING WIN IN PERPIGNAN

Following their home victory against Salford, a trip to the Catalans Dragons would be the Tigers' next destination. Although Catalans had effectively nothing to play for as their place in the Middle 8s Qualifiers had been confirmed, they were always going to be an awkward team to play against on their home ground. Filled with passionate and vocal French supporters, the Stade Gilbert Brutus has not been a happy hunting ground for the Tigers in the past who have lost seven of their last eight matches in Perpignan.

This statistic did not faze the visitors however and they stormed into an early 14-0 lead. An acrobatic finish in the corner by Greg Eden's replacement Jy Hitchcox in the eighth minute and a superb solo effort by Zak Hardaker in the 19th, as well as two Gale conversions and a penalty, had stunned the home side.

The Dragons, rocked by this early assault, did hit back just two minutes later through young half-back Lucas Albert who took a great if slightly forward, offload from forward Julian Bousquet and then through Tony Gigot on 27 minutes. Fouad Yaha then got in on the act five minutes before the break when he was the beneficiary of a flowing move from right to left. As Gigot converted all three tries, the Dragons took an 18-14 lead, something which had looked impossible after the first twenty minutes. As the hooter sounded, the Tigers were awarded a penalty on halfway for a high tackle and Zak Hardaker produced a mighty effort to add the two points. The first-half had been a tale of two halves with the Dragons doing well to stem the Tigers' seemingly unstoppable assault.

The visitors found themselves back in the lead around the 50th minute when a Gale kick was batted back by winger Joel Monaghan into the arms of Greg Minikin who then kicked ahead for himself to score an excellent individual try. Gale's conversion gave the Tigers the slenderest of leads.

Then referee Phil Bentham took centre stage by yellow-carding Castleford substitute Kevin Larroyer on the hour mark for a squirrel grip tackle and then giving Castleford a team warning after three successive penalties.

Ill-discipline saw the visitors reduced to 11 men just seven minutes later as Mike McMeeken was sent to the sin-bin for holding down. Even more controversy followed as Vincent Duport took a well-timed Richard Myler kick to finish in the corner a minute after McMeeken's dismissal. Bentham sent it upstairs and video referee Robert Hicks awarded a penalty try after Hardaker had kicked the ball out of Duport's grasp despite Duport appearing to be in touch before the ball was kicked out and despite Bentham giving a no-try verdict on the field. Gigot converted in front of the posts and the hosts led 24-22 going into the final five minutes.

Cue Jy Hitchcox. An astonishing finish in the corner from the Aussie and a Gale conversion saw Castleford in front by four. In the dying moments, Paul McShane crossed for a scrappy but well-deserved try. A hard-fought victory against the odds in front of a record away following in the south of France was just what the Tigers needed going into the Challenge Cup break.

WHAT THE FANS SAID

@simon030667: "When SL top try scorer gets injured and you replace him with equal quality @ Jybees. That's why we're top of SL. @CTRLFC."

@StueyLeach: "Outstanding win considering what we've had to cope with!!!! Gone through all the emotions during that game but… #WeAreTopOfTheLeague."

@TigerTalkRadio: "After that performance and not getting any decisions… just give us the LLS now we deserve it #champions."

@rosshardyyork: "#COYF awesome 2 points never ever beaten (literally) these days – 40 points little old Cas, what an effort @CTRLFC."

@147_hramsey: "@CTRLFC true warriors to a man, never been more proud, thanks guys."

ADMIRABLE AUGUST

#24 - Brandon Douglas

Date of Birth: 17/08/1997
Height: 188cm (6 ft 2)
Weight: 101kg (15.9 stone)
Nationality: England
Position: Prop/Second-Row
Previous Clubs: Dewsbury Rams (loan), Halifax RLFC (loan)

Brandon joined the Tigers from Bradford Bulls' Scholarship scheme in 2013 before signing a full-time contract in October 2016. He had made his debut a month before away at St Helens where he received the Fans' Man of the Match award despite the heavy 40-16 defeat.

Though Brandon did not take to the field in a Castleford jersey in 2017, he was a frequent performer for Dewsbury and then Halifax, notching over twenty appearances throughout the season. Brandon is a strong runner and his young age of just 20 did not stop him from grappling with forwards such as Gil Dudson of Widnes or Antoni Maria of Leigh in the Middle 8s Qualifiers. Brandon may have missed out on Castleford's 2017, but the future looks bright for Douglas who still has another year left on his contract with the club. Who knows, he may well become an important part of the Tigers' attempt for further glory. If his 2017 is anything to go by, he is certainly ready to show what he can do at the top level.

@SheffieldEagles - 17th April 2017: "40' - Try Dewsbury. 50 seconds remaining of the half and Dewsbury have their second score of the match. Brandon Douglas with it. (16-10)"

@SheffieldEagles - 11th June 2017: "76' - Try Halifax. 50 up for Fax. Brandon Douglas with the try, Tyrer converts. 0-54."

@Halifax_RLFC - 16th July 2017: "7' TRY - Good drives from Douglas and Cahalane set up position. Brandon Moore goes from dummy half and races through the gap to score (0-4)"

TIGERS' UNBEATEN HOME STREAK ENDED BY RESOLUTE SAINTS

Having given his team an extended break after victory in Perpignan secured a top placed regular season finish, coach Daryl Powell would have been dismayed with the performance shelled out by his troops against an in-form St Helens side. The visitors became the first team to beat Castleford at home since last July and inflicted the Tigers' first league defeat in 13 matches.

Despite being camped for most of the first-half on the visitors' line, the Tigers simply could not break through a St Helens defence that withstood a barrage of attacks. Then, approaching midway through the first-half, in a rare jaunt into the Castleford half, second-rower Zeb Taia took advantage of some weak tackling to register the first points of the night. Centre Mark Percival converted and then saints extended their lead to eight with a penalty five minutes later. Both sides were victims of the video referee as Kyle Amor had a try chalked off for the visitors for a knock-on, whilst the Tigers had a great opportunistic try rejected for offside.

0-8 down, the hosts had to hit back first after the break. They did just that as Adam Milner barged his way over from dummy-half on 48 minutes. Luke Gale's conversion reduced the deficit to two points. But St Helens surged back when Jonny Lomax's short pass set up Roby six minutes later after some poor tackling had enabled prop, Luke Thompson, to charge down the middle of the field. 13 minutes later, Lomax pounced on a bobbling ball from substitute Matty Smith's low kick, the half-back restored to the Saints 17 after a horrendous eye injury.

With 13 minutes left and the hosts 20-6 down, the game looked to be in the visitors' hands. Joel Monaghan's one-handed dive in the right-hand corner did give the Tigers hope with eight minutes to go before Roby muscled his way over in the 75th minute from close range to secure what was effectively a convincing victory for the Saints who

moved third in Super League.

The Tigers were below par and despite dominating territory and the ball could only notch up two tries. Their left-sided attack seemed heavily disjointed and was unable to break through the staunch St Helens defence. It was a terrible start to the Super 8s for the Tigers; improvement was much needed if they were going to secure the League Leaders' Shield soon. No doubt about it, this improvement came in truckloads.

WHAT THE FANS SAID

@SirJackWest: "All well and good winning 12 in a row but if you don't turn up in the Super 8s we'll achieve nothing."

@scottygarman: "We were poor but Saints' defence at times was unreal. No complaints."

@markhudson2205: "Credit to @Saints1890 that was some performance. Still 10 points clear but hurting tonight."

@seanbetts1: "I thought they looked a good way in front of us tonight in all aspects of the game."

@Paulctsc: "Didn't click tonight against a very good Saints team. Lots of positives from the returning players, Salford next."

JUNIOR MOORS SIGNS ONE-YEAR CONTRACT EXTENSION UNTIL THE END OF 2020

Junior had already signed a two-year contract extension in October 2016, therefore the news of another extension was a tad surprising yet brilliant news for Castleford fans. 2016 and 2017 had shown Junior's class. He has the ability to fend off numerous defenders, draw men in and then throw out wonderful offloads which are always a pleasure to watch. His injuries, however, have in the past resulted in him being sidelined for long periods of time. He was out for eight weeks with a knee injury sustained in the home win over Warrington in June. Yet when he takes to the field, his impact is like no other. In 2017, just his presence scared defenders and roused the Castleford fans and his hard work and powerful running earned him a new extension to his 2018 and 2019 contract.

Junior was always laid back when talking about his new contract but paid tribute to his fellow players, coaches and the fans who welcomed him and his family to the club: "I'm over the moon, I've really enjoyed my time here, we have a great bunch of blokes here at Castleford and great coaching staff so it was a really easy decision to make. I've been here for three years now and the fans have been outstanding every year, and it's great to see them enjoying us going so well this season."

Asked whether he would stay on after this deal and remain a Tiger for the rest of his career, Moors said: "My family are enjoying it and I'm enjoying it here so I'd be keen to stay on."

Powell waxed lyrical about Junior's ability on the field and his improvements since he first joined, but also highlighted how important it is for the club that its best players still want to remain at the Tigers: "Junior Moors is a high-quality player who has continued to get better during his time at the club. His ability as a ballplayer in the middle of the field is outstanding as is his ball carrying strength,"

Powell added: "The fact that our best players continue to extend their contracts is a huge compliment to the club and its direction at the moment. Junior's extension shows this again and I am so pleased I will be able to work with him on a continued basis."

#25 - Jy Hitchcox

Date of Birth: 18/08/1989
Height: 177cm (5 ft 8)
Weight: 88kg (13.9 stone)
Country: Australia
Position: Wing
Previous Clubs: Wests Tigers, Featherstone Rovers, Batley Bulldogs (loan)

Appearances: 10	**Avg. Gain:** 7.57
Tries: 3	**Tackles:** 44
Try Assists: 1	**Clean Breaks:** 4
Metres: 825	**Offloads:** 10

Jy moved to the club from Featherstone Rovers in 2016 after a brief stint at NRL side Wests Tigers. Jy played nine games in 2016 scoring seven tries including a dream two-try debut away at Hull FC. In doing so, he did enough to secure a two-year contract until the end of 2018.

His 2016 was however ruined by hand and knee injuries that restricted his game time. With rumours of a career-threatening knee injury, it was later confirmed Jy had a rare bone disease. It was a miracle that he appeared at all in 2017. But after playing in two games for his loan side Batley in April, Jy made his long-awaited comeback for the Tigers. He looked like he had never been away as he made three try-saving tackles on St Helens winger Regan Grace to help a much-changed Castleford side triumph 16-12. Jy continued to flourish on the wing and was seriously unlucky not to get more games under his belt in 2017, often losing his place to the equally impressive Greg Minikin.

Jy's standout performance of 2017 was undoubtedly his two-try performance away at Catalans in July. Both of his tries demonstrated his outstanding turn of pace and his ability to finish spectacularly. When Jy did pull on the Tigers jersey in 2017, he did not disappoint. Jy, despite his small stature, asserted himself as a brilliant catcher of the ball whilst his fast and fancy footwork often fooled defences as he drove the ball away from his line. Despite playing only ten games in 2017, Jy was an essential part of the squad and whenever called upon, he took his opportunity with both hands. He would go on to play in Castleford's maiden Grand Final as Greg Eden moved to fullback in the absence of Zak Hardaker and stood up well.

The 2017 competition between Hitchcox and Minikin for the right-wing was fascinating. With a full pre-season and Jy's nightmarish injuries behind him, this battle could be even closer in 2018.

@briggsySRD90 – 22nd July 2017: "Jy Hitchcox with one of the best finishes you will see for a long time! Fair play #SLCatCas."
@josh42217 – 22nd July 2017: "Seen some tries but that Hitchcox try was up there as one of the best I've ever seen #COYF."
@AaronBower – 4th June 2017: "Jy Hitchcox has been brilliant for Castleford. Three great tackles to deny the Saints tries, including a great one on Percival then."

TIGERS HAVE ONE HAND ON LEAGUE LEADERS' SHIELD AFTER BRUSHING ASIDE THE RED DEVILS

It was imperative for the Tigers to 'get back on the horse' following their disappointing defeat to St Helens the previous week. This fixture, although the Tigers had already lost to the Red Devils away from home this season, provided a great opportunity to do so as the hosts had lost eight of their previous nine matches.

The Red Devils, giving a home debut to New Zealand international Manu Vatuvei, nicknamed "The Beast" for quite obvious reasons, threatened the Tigers line repeatedly early on. A sixth minute Ryan Lannon try was disallowed for obstruction which seemed harsh sparking the home fans into expressing their annoyance. This annoyance grew as merely a minute later Zak Hardaker followed up a break by talismanic hooker Paul McShane to score under the posts.

Both sides had tries disallowed by the video referee before Hardaker got his second when he hit a fantastic line to take a well-timed pass from winger Jy Hitchcox, rounding Salford fullback Niall Evalds on his way to the line. Gale's conversions meant the score was 12-0 at the break.

Within three minutes of the restart, Salford scored their first points thanks to a great finish by Vatuvei who somehow managed to ground a Todd Carney grubber before the ball went dead. Castleford withstood tremendous pressure to survive a further reduction of arrears with the visitors themselves being the next scorers. A brilliant dummy by McShane fooled the Salford defence on the hour mark. And with 15 minutes left, the Tigers scored a trademark try to put the game to bed. Hardaker broke through out on the right to feed his supporting halfback Gale who was brought to ground, but not tackled. Gale returned the ball to Hardaker who launched a huge pass to winger Hitchcox for the

score of the game. Gale missed his first conversion of the night but succeeded with a drop-goal with five minutes remaining to make it 23-4.

In bad weather, Castleford at times struggled to keep hold of the ball whilst discipline was again an issue. Yet with another vital two points and with second-placed Leeds losing to Wakefield the night before, Castleford now just needed a win or a draw in next week's match against, ironically the team that relegated them twice in the 2000s, Trinity, to lift the League Leaders' Shield and finish top for the first time in their history.

WHAT THE FANS SAID

@HantsCastiger: "First watched @CTRLFC 36 years ago. Never ever thought I would witness a season like this. You lads are history makers – so proud #coyf."

@James27LUFC: "Bubble well and truly inflated… again."

@Diddididi64: "10 points clear, 10 to play for and a massive points difference in our favour mmmmmmmm."

@SeanWilson85: "10 points clear with 5 games to go. Unbelievable."

@pontytiger: "I used to love to hate @ mcshane_paul now I'm just totally in love with him."

#26 - Kieran Gill

Date of Birth: 04/12/1995
Height: 190cm (6 ft 2)
Weight: 85kg (13.4 stone)
Country: England
Position: Centre/Wing
Previous Clubs: Salford Red Devils, Oxford RL (loan), Oldham Roughyeds (loan)

Appearances: 1	**Avg. Gain:** 4.00
Tries: 1	**Tackles:** 3
Try Assists: 0	**Clean Breaks:** 1
Metres: 32	**Offloads:** 1

Kieran, having first been in Castleford's academy at a young age only to be released and join Salford's, returned to join the Tigers in 2015. Gill, now aged just 21, was rewarded at 19 with a professional contract and has been in and around the first-team set-up ever since.

In 2016 he was sent on loan first to Oxford, then to Oldham Roughyeds where he played a key role in Oldham's ascent to sixth in the Championship. In 2017 he was again sent on loan to Oldham where he impressed further for the club from across the Pennines scoring five tries in nine games. Kieran was then recalled for Castleford's game against St Helens in June just three days prior to signing his new one-year contract. It must be said that Kieran did not look out of place at all in the first-team. And being a Castleford fan himself, his dream to just get onto the field was made even more surreal when he scored a well-taken try in the first half. Kieran, unfortunately, suffered a season-ending injury in the early stages of the game but carried on with a warrior-like determination even going on to score his try before he simply could go on no longer and had to leave the field.

Despite only making the one appearance for the Tigers in 2017, the way in which he genuinely looked comfortable at the highest level, how determined he was to do his share of defending and how he took numerous drives forward despite being injured displayed the lengths Kieran would go in order to help his team and the club. This demonstration of such spirit and resolve by Kieran to try to carry on through the pain barrier epitomised the Tigers in general in 2017; whoever took to the field would not let his teammates down. It is this sort of culture, instilled in the team by Powell, that breeds winners and success. Hopefully, with a decent pre-season and a complete recovery from injury, Kieran can show his true potential in 2018.

@CTRLFC - 4th June 2017: "FT: Castleford Tigers 16-12 St. Helens...Tries from Kieran Gill, Mike McMeeken and Tom Holmes give the Tigers a great victory over the Saints."
@TheChallengeCup - 18th March 2017: "A Castleford-esque try from loanee Kieran Gill as he darts down the left wing to score for @Roughyeds. OLD 36-8 HAY."

REMEMBER THE DATE: CASTLEFORD MAKE HISTORY

A warm, pleasant evening greeted the Mend-a-Hose Jungle as Castleford Tigers hosted their local rivals, Wakefield Trinity, in a highly-anticipated clash that saw the Tigers finally crowned as deserved league leaders.

In their 91-year history, Castleford have never had a team that has finished top of the league, whether that be the old First Division or the 1996-founded Super League. Their last trophy was the Regal Trophy 23 years ago. Last Thursday night, these pieces of unwanted history were destroyed forever as the Tigers dispatched Trinity with relative ease to lift the League Leaders' Shield in front of the Sky cameras and in full view of their long-suffering fans.

Prior to this momentous event, 2017 had already been and will still be considered as one of the most exciting Super League competitions yet and for one reason: The Tigers. Lighting up the league, and the sport in general, Castleford Tigers upset the apple cart so much that there were no apples left to disturb. They defied their critics who assuredly proclaimed that "the wheels would fall off" eventually. But with a ten-point advantage over second-placed Leeds Rhinos going into this the third Super 8s game, the Tigers' wheels were well and truly fixed on.

The potential to secure the league leaders title in this fixture: a home tie where the Castleford fans are renowned for their vociferous and passionate backing of their team against their arch-rivals and the team that relegated them in both 2004 and 2006, was surely too good to be true. Say that to Daryl Powell and his chargers.

Castleford were understandably nervous in the opening exchanges as Greg Minikin and Tigers stalwart Jake Webster came up with uncharacteristic mistakes. Liam Finn nudged the visitors ahead with a penalty goal after Luke Gale hit Trinity full-back Max Jowitt around the head.

On nine minutes, however, Castleford struck with attacking vigour, a common occurrence in almost every game the Tigers played in 2017, as Zak Hardaker slid over for a well-taken try. Luke Gale converted to make it 6-2.

But this kicked Trinity back into life and they responded just six minutes later as Dean Hadley, deputising at hooker in place of the recently impressive, but injured, Kyle Wood, fed Reece Lyne who sent winger Ben Jones-Bishop in at the corner. As Finn missed the conversion, the scores remained level.

It took just five minutes for the Tigers to reply midway through the first-half as, on the back of a cheeky one-on-one rip by Paul McShane on the colossal David Fifita, Mike McMeeken somehow stretched out of three tacklers to reach for the line. Although referee James Child claimed a no-try on the field, video referee Phil Bentham overturned his decision, albeit with many replays, on the clear evidence that McMeeken's remarkable stretch had, in fact, touched the whitewash.

The home fans were by now in a joyous mood, and the atmosphere became even more raucous just past the half-hour mark when Hardaker again showed his classy credentials with a wonderful run out of nothing to create an opening for Webster to hold off two defenders and cross for his first of the night. With a near-capacity crowd of 11,235, the overwhelming

majority being Castleford fans, the ground descended into raptures as daylight, courtesy of an 18-6 lead as Gale converted all three efforts, was finally established between the two teams.

The champagne was put on ice however as Trinity hit back again just a minute before the break. Mason Caton-Brown, playing centre in place of the injured Joe Arundel, burrowed his way through soft defence to bring Trinity back into the contest at just the right time.

Wakefield were also the first team to score following the break as captain Danny Kirmond stepped out of some more poor tackling to bring his side back to within four points. With Finn converting, the visitors were only two points behind and there appeared to be tension in the air at the Jungle for the first time during the game.

Four minutes later, these fears were quelled as a devastating spell saw the Tigers open up a 34-16 lead. First, Greg Eden, returning from what had initially been feared as a season-ending injury, collected a superb cut-out pass from scrum-half Luke Gale to score his 35th Super League try of 2017.

Then just three minutes later, Webster got his second after Bill Tupou had knocked down Hardaker's pass as he looked to find the former New Zealand international. Webster, a popular figure amongst the Castleford faithful, completed his first ever hat-trick in the English game on the 63rd minute as he stormed onto a well-timed Roberts pass. Just two minutes after Webster's exploits, Gale slotted over a drop-goal to open up a four-try lead.

With ten minutes to go, Webster then recorded a memorable fourth as he again charged onto a pass, this time from the equally impressive McMeeken. Trinity would not lie down though and scored a consolation as Max Jowitt, who showed up well in place of the injured Scott Grix, pounced on a Tupou offload with eight minutes to go.

The Tigers were however determined to be the last on the scoresheet on this historic night and they achieved that when Zak Hardaker supported a break by, yes that man Jake Webster, to record his second of the night. Gale's conversion left the scores 45-20 and this is how it would stay until James Child called time.

Cue elation. The Castleford fans could not, and still many do not, believe what they had witnessed on this night and in 2017 in general. As the name of each player was called up to the podium from where the Shield would be held aloft, cheers from every corner of the

17th August 2017 - Super 8s Round 3 Castleford 45-20 Wakefield Trinity

"old girl", as Castleford Tigers' chief executive Steve Gill calls the stadium, greeted the announcement. Sheer pride and euphoria exploded into a deafening boom as captain Michael Shenton, a long-term Castleford player and fan, lifted the Shield into the air.

The fireworks that greeted this gesture were reminiscent of how the Tigers had lit up the Super League season as a whole and as Sweet Caroline, the adopted victory anthem for the club ever since the famous Luke Dorn winning try against Wigan in 2014, was belted over the sound system and around the stadium, many Castleford fans began to dream whether the "big one", the Grand Final, was a possibility too. After all, all that stood between the Tigers and Old Trafford was a home semi-final. Backed by their dedicated fans, the Tigers had lost only once since July 2016 at home, soon to be twice. A fortress is what awaited any challenger that arrived on Thursday 28 September.

WHAT THE FANS SAID

@bethmaidurant: "So unbelievably proud of @ CTRLFC this evening. 20 years watching this little mining town club – through relegations and tears to this!"

@CasFaithful: "It's for us fans, it's for the board, it's for the players and it's for Powell, but most importantly, this is for you Jack! Thank you!!"

@Ender83: "Fantastic evening watching @ CTRLFC lift the League Leaders' shield tonight!! Let's hope we can now get to the grand final!"

@MellJeffery: "What a day! My eldest gets to go Uni. of Lincoln to study chemistry and @CTRLFC win league leaders shield ... lots of tears (of joy) today!"

@tom_alexander69: "Was there to see them relegated twice, promoted twice and now see them lift the league leaders shield, bring on the Aussies #ClassyCas."

@jimb02511: "2013 – 30 mins away from adminstration. 2017 – League' Leaders Shield winners and qualifying for world club series. ALL CAS ARE WE!"

JOE WARDLE SIGNS FOR CASTLEFORD ON A THREE-YEAR DEAL

The game's worst-kept secret was outed with the news that Joe Wardle, who was then plying his trade with Newcastle Knights in Australia, had signed a three-year contract with the Tigers. Rumoured to have been joining the club since the spring, it was like a weight had been lifted off Castleford fans' shoulders with the news.

Joe, a Scottish international with six caps to his name, will mostly be remembered for his six-year stint at Huddersfield Giants where he played 141 appearances before he left Britain for Australia in December 2016 to join up with the Newcastle Knights on a three-year deal. Joe, however, started his career at Bradford Bulls where he progressed through its academy setup after signing from amateur club Illingworth ARLFC. He made his first appearance in May 2010 in a Challenge Cup game against Warrington Wolves and would feature ten times over the course of the season. It was in September of that year that he rejected a new Bradford deal and signed for the Giants.

His time at the Knights was marred by homesickness. After playing 17 games in which he scored four tries, Wardle secured a release from his contract to sign for the Tigers on a three-year deal ahead of the 2018 season.

Joe was humble in reference to his old club in Australia but outlined how excited he was to be coming back home and to the Tigers in particular: "I would just like to say thank you to Newcastle for working alongside me in what has been a hard time adjusting to life down under. Rugby careers are short so happiness is key and sometimes things don't work out, which is, unfortunately, the case. I am really looking forward to getting back home, getting my family settled and teaming up with Daryl and the rest of the boys for the 2018 campaign."

Powell declared how long he had been an admirer of Joe and to the extent to which he can improve the already-impressive Tigers squad: "Joe Wardle is a player that I have been a fan of for a number of years since his time at Huddersfield. I am delighted that on returning to England, he has decided that we are the club to help him achieve his goals in the game."

Powell added: "He is a tough player on both sides of the game, being a great line runner on attack, and a solid, aggressive defender. He can play in both centre and back-row positions which strengthens us significantly and grows our competition for places within an already awesome squad. I look forward to his arrival at the club and getting him accustomed to how we play."

Time will tell whether Joe can adapt to the Tigers' venerated style of play, but his strong ball-carrying and assertive defence look set to bring yet another dimension to the Castleford team that rightly won so many plaudits in 2017.

GRANT MILLINGTON SIGNS THREE-YEAR CONTRACT EXTENSION UNTIL THE END OF 2020

Ah, Grant Millington. The word legend gets bandied about too much, but 'Millo' typifies the word in all its glory. Massively underrated, the transformation of himself as a player from when he first joined back in 2012 from Canterbury Bulldogs to where he is now is enormous. Grant has become an integral part of the Tigers, both on and off the field. He is unanimously respected and his rugby brain is second to none.

Grant started his career at the Cronulla Sharks where he spent three seasons and registered just shy of 50 appearances for the club. In the 2010 season, Grant played in all but one of that year's games. From there, he went to Canterbury ahead of the 2011 season, but injury reduced his appearance tally to seven. Grant was contracted to the Bulldogs for the 2012 season but was granted an early release to join the Tigers who were managed by then-coach Ian Millward. Since then, Grant has played over 150 times for the West Yorkshire club.

Upon signing the extension, Grant explained how he sees his future firmly at the Tigers and spoke of his joy at being part of the club's transformation: "The club has been fantastic to me and my family. We love it here at Cas and this is home for us."

Millington added: "I don't think I could play for any other club. The club has transformed on and off the pitch since I joined and I'm proud to be a part of that."

Powell stated just how important Grant had been for the Tigers up to this point and how he would be in the future: "Grant Millington has been outstanding again this season and I'm delighted that he has agreed to extend his contract to remain with the Tigers. His skill sets are second to none as a front row player and he has been integral to the way we have played the game over the last few years."

Powell added: "I am confident that he will continue to improve and help to drive our standards for the remainder of this year and beyond."

Adrian Vowles takes some beating, but Grant is surely one of Castleford's best ever imports.

SMASHING SEPTEMBER

#27 - Tuoyo Egodo

Date of Birth: 16/02/1997
Height: 178cm (5 ft 8)
Weight: 96kg (15.1 stone)
Country: England
Position: Centre/Wing
Previous Clubs: London Broncos, Hemel Stags (loan), Oldham Roughyeds (loan), York City Knights (loan)

Appearances: 1   **Avg. Gain:** 5.71
Tries: 3   **Tackles:** 5
Try Assists: 0   **Clean Breaks:** 3
Metres: 97   **Offloads:** 0

Tuoyo, before signing with the Tigers in October 2016 on a two-year deal, had spent the previous three years with the Broncos' academy where he was sent on loan to League 1 side Hemel Stags in 2016. Impressing when he took to the field, Tuoyo scored one try in nine games. In 2017, the Londoner featured ten times for Oldham and twice for York, proving a big hit with both sets of fans because of his direct and powerful running, as well as his bone-crushing defence.

It was a pleasure to see Tuoyo and Kieran Gill playing alongside each other for the Roughyeds and being vital in aiding each other's progress before Kieran suffered his injury. At just 20 years of age, Tuoyo was given the responsibility by Powell to occupy a wing berth at home to Hull FC in the Tigers' last home game of the Super 8s. Although the result was a great disappointment, a 48-16 hammering, Tuoyo could hold his head up high. After a shaky start where he made a few mistakes, the 20-year-old quickly grew into the game and provided a potent threat when driving the ball out of defence as well as holding his own against his opposite number, Fetuli Talanoa. His combination with Greg Eden, who was operating at full-back, and his centre Jake Webster, appeared seamless with Tuoyo slotting straight into the position usually occupied by Greg Minikin. And in doing so, he emerged from the game with a well-taken hat-trick.

From his debut outing, it was evident that Tuoyo has a big future ahead of him and may well turn into the next gem unearthed by Daryl Powell and his coaching staff. With consistent performances for Oldham and this appearance for the Tigers under his belt in 2017, Tuoyo can only improve and grow in confidence. 2018 could be the time for the ex-London starlet to announce himself onto the Rugby League stage.

@rosshmediaman – 22nd September 2017: "Some debut this from young Tuoyo Egodo. His hat-trick try has got Cas right back in the game at 28-16 with 30 minutes remaining. #SLCasHul."
@MikePreston92 – 22nd September 2017: "So pleased for @TEGOD97 hope you remember that for years to come."
@CTRLFC – 22nd September 2017: "TRY CAS!!! HAT-TRICK FOR EGODO!! What a debut for the youngster."

TIGERS WITHSTAND A STUBBORN GIANTS PERFORMANCE TO MAKE IT EIGHT WINS FROM NINE

Daryl Powell spoke in the week leading up to this clash that Huddersfield Giants would be a "desperate" team who were vying for that fourth and final play-off spot. The hosts certainly lived up to this billing as they led 12-6 at half-time after a tough first forty minutes for the Tigers. But buoyed by their memorable win over Wakefield Trinity to finish top for the first time in their 91-year history, the Tigers refused to put the cue on the rack and made it eight wins from nine.

The first-half was a very tight affair and it wasn't until the 12th minute when Jake Webster, playing his 200th career appearance in the British game, stormed onto a well-timed Ben Roberts pass to crash over in customary style. Luke Gale converted, as he did for all four of the Tigers' tries to take him past the 300-point mark for the season, to make it 6-0. Huddersfield however, determined to continue their recent good form, sprang to life and only a stunning tackle by Tigers favourite Jesse Sene-Lefao stopped winger Jermaine McGillvary, who was also making his 200th career appearance, from scoring in the corner. But after yet another devastating run by Giants' prop Sebastine Ikahihifo, the Castleford defence could not stop Oliver Roberts charging over from a Danny Brough pass in the 22nd minute. Brough missed the relatively simple kick to leave the Tigers in front. Just six minutes before half-time, Huddersfield struck once more, this time through Paul Clough. Brough had clearly annoyed his coach Rick Stone with his first wayward conversion attempt as Jordan Rankin, the beneficiary of a new three-year deal with the Giants in the week leading up to the game, took over the kicking duties and duly obliged to leave the hosts 10-6 up. Barely seconds before the hooter Huddersfield stretched their lead by a further two points as Jordan Rankin added a penalty after hooker Kruise Leeming was taken out off of the ball by a Tigers player.

Whatever Powell said at half-time clearly worked. Just three minutes into the second forty, Ben Roberts showed his silky skills to spot a hole in the Giants' defence for a great individual try. The scores were level as Gale kicked his second of the night. And just nine minutes later, the Tigers were in again. Eden, taking his league tally to 36 for the season, was the grateful recipient of fine link-up play between Gale and Hardaker. Gale's conversion from the touchline was superb and the Tigers hit the front at18-12. Eden then returned the favour to Gale just ten minutes later as the former bested his opposite winger McGillvary to feed his scrum-half on the inside to take the visitors out of sight.

Although Darnell McIntosh grabbed a try just three minutes before the end, it was a mere consolation as Rankin's missed conversion attempt meant the Giants still needed two scores to win.

Before the game, it was a question of whether Castleford could maintain their focus and momentum after the elation of the game two weeks ago. This hard-fought victory, their fifth in succession over the Giants, emphatically put that question to bed.

WHAT THE FANS SAID

@PeterOsbornCas:
"Good win tonight. Could have bottled it at half time but we got stuck in. Alex Foster was brilliant #COYF."

@WWWoodzy92:
"Showing our class it seems!! Players playing for a spot in the semi final team! This is what we want #COYF."

@jackappo1993:
"Well a win is a win, well played Cas #COYF."

@Paulctsc: "Although not at our best last night, to step up a gear and take the game away from Huddersfield was outstanding. #COYF."

@cwalker_1995:
"Great win for the Tigers against a team that is chasing the top four! #coyf."

CASTLEFORD ANNOUNCE ANNUAL PROFIT OF £286,052 FOR 2016

Being one of the perennial strugglers, not just on the field, but off it too, Castleford's bank balance has not always been a healthy one. In 2013 Steve Gill took over as Chief Executive. After being 24 hours away from administration, the club has been on an upward turn ever since. Daryl Powell's injection of life midway through the 2013 season inspired hope. Hope turned into reality in 2014 when the Tigers walked out at Wembley for the first time since their defeat to Wigan in 1992. And after having Chairman Jack Fulton to thank for the club simply being kept alive, it brought tears to most Castleford fans' eyes to witness this hero being pushed out onto the Wembley turf in a wheelchair by son Ian, now Chairman after Jack's sad passing in September 2015.

From then on, the financial outlook of the club has remained positive, even to the point at which Castleford have become one of the very few clubs to actually record a turnover in profit. On the back of a wonderful 2014, the club recorded a profit of £445,000 for that financial year, a huge transformation from the dark days of 2013. Such stability has continued as this recent news demonstrated.

For the 2016 financial year, the club announced that their annual turnover was up over £0.5 million, giving Castleford an overall turnover of £4.6 million. That turnover generated an overall profit of £286,052. This profit, according to the club, enabled the Tigers to invest heavily in their 2017 playing and coaching squads.

Chairman Ian Fulton thanked all those associated with the club for contributing to the club now being a successful business: "This is the third consecutive year that Castleford Tigers has not received any financial assistance, as we continue to strive to be a lean and well run Rugby League club. I'd like to take this opportunity to thank all of our club staff, club sponsors, volunteers and of course I'd like to thank our supporters for helping us achieve this."

Such a profit should surely grow on the back of such a memorable and thrilling season.

#28 - Conor Fitzsimmons

Date of Birth: 01/05/1998
Height: 185cm (6 ft 1)
Weight: 97kg (15.3 stone)
Country: England
Position: Loose Forward/ Second Row
Previous Clubs: Workington Town (loan)
National Honours: 3 caps for England
Academy

Conor joined the Tigers in June 2015 from the Cumbria RFL Academy on an initial trial basis, but the forward soon impressed his coaches and was rewarded with an 18-month contract. Conor then went on to make his first-team debut for the Tigers during 2016, coming off of the bench against St Helens in May. Conor was a regular in the Tigers under 19s side in 2015 and 2016 and through his good form, earned himself a place in England's Academy side for their summer 2016 tour of Australia.

Although failing to register a first-team appearance for the Tigers in 2017, Conor spent the season on loan at Workington Town where he linked up with Dave Clark who coached him during his time at the Cumbria RFL Academy. While at Workington, Conor was a regular figure on the field, notching up 22 appearances and displaying a maturity that belied his youthful age.

At Castleford's last home game in the semi-final against St Helens, coach Daryl Powell confirmed that Conor would be leaving the club at the end of the 2017 season. It is a shame that Conor never got to establish himself in the Tigers' pack, but with the first-team forwards excelling in 2017, his chances of doing so were extremely limited. Every Castleford fan would like to wish Conor well in his future endeavours.

@WorkingtonTown - 5th February 2017: "TOWN TRY! Conor Fitzsimmons caps off a great debut by touching down after Dowsett's magnificent flicked pass under the sticks."

@Doncaster_RLFC - 4th June 2017: "8' Try Workington. A good kick through is pounced upon by Conor Fitzsimmons for the home side's first try. 4-6 #COYD"

@Doncaster_RLFC - 20th August 2017: "53' Try Workington. They move the ball to the right and Fitzsimmons forces his way over. 20-15 #COYD"

TIGERS CRUISE TO YET ANOTHER VICTORY OVER LEEDS

Eight wins in a row and four league victories in 2017 against their big-city rivals was the prize for the Tigers heading into this match. With Leeds only needing one more point to assure themselves of a second-placed finish and with Castleford already assured of a home semi-final, one could have predicted that the visitors may well have caused the Tigers much more trouble than they did. The scoreline flattered the Rhinos, who scored three tries when the game was already dead and buried.

Castleford fell to an early 0-6 deficit as Kallum Watkins powered through opposite number Michael Shenton in the sixth minute. This was to be the catalyst for 30 unanswered points from the hosts. First, Greg Eden registered his 37th try of the season, finishing off a sweeping move from right to left in the 13th minute. It took another 11 minutes for Ben Roberts to score his first of two with a classy try that resembled a hot knife through butter.

By now the floodgates were opening and centre Jake Webster, scoring his sixth try in three games, powered onto a short Paul McShane pass on 28 minutes. The Tigers were now red hot and it took only three more minutes for Alex Foster, a Leeds Rhinos academy product, to notch up his first try in Castleford colours, showing brute strength to force his way over the line after Rhinos fullback, Jack Walker had failed to deal with a Gale bomb. Roberts had his second three minutes before the break when he latched onto a Gale grubber kick that fooled the visitors' defence. Gale converted all five tries and the hosts were out of sight at 30-6.

Leeds had to be the first to score following the restart and they were when Jamie Jones-Buchanan benefitted from a switched-off Castleford defence from a scrum to power over on 45 minutes. This scrum had resulted from a Greg Minikin knock-on. The winger was to atone for his error three minutes later after being sent in by Webster. 36-12 and the game was effectively over. Leeds hooker Matt Parcell would score on 65 minutes and Mitch Garbutt as the hooter sounded, but the scoreline flattered the visitors.

A potential Grand Final rehearsal, Castleford appeared able to punch holes through the Rhinos' defence with ease. Worryingly for the Tigers, Ben Roberts did not reappear after

half-time and Zak Hardaker looked to be in heaps of pain as he left the field after Parcell's effort. Thankfully, both would not take too much time out of the team and would return for the vital games to come. This was an eighth win against Leeds in succession and left the Tigers with a 12-point margin at the top of the table.

A trip to Wigan, who were involved in the exciting hunt for those last two elusive top four places, beckoned for the Tigers. And although Hardaker was deemed fit to play, Roberts and Luke Gale, who in the week leading up to the Wigan game was recovering from an appendix operation, were missing. The Tigers would have to do it tough.

WHAT THE FANS SAID

@JoshCheetham91:
"The points difference is frightening. We really have been head and shoulders above everybody this season. Incredible #COYF."

@ClarkstonSte: "RECORD BREAKER! Congratulations to @snozzer_gale, scored the most points in a @CTRLFC season, breaking Bob Beardmore's 33 year record #COYF."

@JoshCheetham91:
"The points difference is frightening. We really have been head and shoulders above everybody this season. Incredible #COYF."

@JoshCheetham91:
"The points difference is frightening. We really have been head and shoulders above everybody this season. Incredible #COYF."

@JoshCheetham91:
"The points difference is frightening. We really have been head and shoulders above everybody this season. Incredible #COYF."

TOM HOLMES JOINS FEATHERSTONE ROVERS ON ONE-YEAR DEAL AT THE END OF THE SEASON

Castleford fans greeted this news with a great deal of sadness. Having come through the ranks at the Tigers after joining the Tigers scholarship scheme as a 14-year old, he went on to captain the Tigers academy team before making the step up to the first-team squad. Tom made his first-team debut for the Tigers back in 2015 but has since found opportunities hard to come by in 2017, making just six appearances during the 2017 season. However, in those six appearances, he demonstrated that he was a capable Super League quality player.

Tom was actually under contract for the 2018 season but felt it was necessary that he looked elsewhere for regular first-team rugby. Being behind both Ben Roberts and Luke Gale in the Tigers' stellar 2017 season and likely to stay there for the next few years, Tom was eager to progress in an environment where game time was not at a premium: "I've loved my time here at Castleford since I joined my hometown club as a 14-year-old boy. Obviously, it's been tough for me to get into the squad here this season with two of the best half-backs in the league here in Luke Gale and Ben Roberts. Getting game time now for me, at this point in my career, is crucial. I did have offers from another Super League club, but Championship for me right now, where I can play week in week out is the best option for me to progress my career.

Holmes added: "Castleford Tigers has been home to me now for such a long time and I will be forever grateful to everyone at the club for helping me progress in my career. I have had the opportunity to work with some amazing players and coaches during my time here and I have learnt so much. But for my development, and with me only being 21, getting week-in-week-out game time is what I need. I've still got a long career ahead of me and I would love to return to Castleford Tigers at some point in the future. I'd like to thank everyone here at Castleford for supporting my development, especially the Tigers fans who make this club what it is."

Powell also wished Tom all the best for next season and totally understood his decision to move on: "This is a great opportunity for Tom to play regular Rugby League in the Championship. Tom has been developing within our system for a few years now and has played a number of first-team games where he has acquitted himself really well. However, we feel now is the right time for him to focus on playing weekly in the Championship environment. We would like to wish Tom all the best for next season and thank him for his time with Castleford Tigers."

All Castleford fans wish Tom the best for 2018 and hope, in his own words, that one day he will return to the club where he had, by the end of 2017, spent a third of his life playing.

LUKE GALE WINS ALBERT GOLDTHORPE MEDAL FOR THIRD YEAR RUNNING

Luke Gale was named the winner of the Albert Goldthorpe Medal two games before the end of the Super 8s. The Medal is awarded by League Express. Reporters for the newspaper cast their votes based on which player they believe has been the best but also the fairest player on the pitch. Three points, two points and one point are awarded to the top three players respectively.

The former Doncaster, London and Bradford scrum-half had been in inspired form yet again for the Tigers and orchestrated the club to their first ever top-placed finish and first ever Grand Final.

League Express editor Martyn Sadler spoke highly of Luke Gale and the role that the Castleford coaching staff have played in Gale's development: "It's been an astonishing rise to prominence for the Castleford half-back, who joined the Tigers from Bradford Bulls in 2015 after three years at Odsal and three years with Harlequins, as London Broncos were then called, between 2009 and 2011.

"It was under Daryl Powell at Castleford that Gale's career really took off. And I'm sure that's because Powell's assistants, Danny Orr and Ryan Sheridan, who had both been fine half-backs themselves, were able to give him the guidance he needed at the Jungle. Without their influence, I suspect that he wouldn't be the player he is today."

The way in which Luke is impressing as every season passes, there is no reason why he cannot win it for a record-fourth time in 2018.

LUKE GALE POTENTIALLY OUT FOR THE SEASON AFTER AN APPENDIX OPERATION

The Tigers were hit with the devastating news that Luke Gale was potentially out for the season after an appendix operation. The club said he had been experiencing pain the day before his operation and went to the hospital for it to be checked out only to be given the awful prognosis that Gale faced weeks and potentially months on the sideline.

Luke Gale spoke before his operation with a heavy heart but emphasised that he was determined to get back on the field before the season's end: "I'm absolutely gutted to be facing surgery at this point in the season. This is a freak situation that could happen to anyone at any time and it's just really unfortunate for me that it has happened to me now at such a crucial point in the season. Rest assured I'll be doing all I can to aid my recovery with an aim to getting back on the pitch as soon as possible. In the meantime, I'll be 100% behind my teammates in our quest for the Grand Final to top off what has already been a fantastic year."

Powell also echoed Luke's desire to get back on the field before the Grand Final or even the semi-final: "Luke has had surgery relating to his appendix this afternoon which will keep him out of immediate action on the field. We are hoping for a speedy recovery back to the field before the end of the season."

The news could not have come at a worse time for Castleford; with two weeks to go until their home semi-final for a place in the Grand Final, this was a cruel twist of fate.

DARYL POWELL ANNOUNCES PLAYERS TO LEAVE AT THE END OF THE 2017 SEASON

At Castleford's annual awards ceremony at Elland Road, coach Powell confirmed that Kevin Larroyer, Joel Monaghan, Tom Holmes, and Luke Million would all be leaving the club at the end of the 2017 season. Powell would later, after the home semi-final win over St Helens, announce that Conor Fitzsimmons was to move on from the club at the end of the year.

Million and Fitzsimmons, whilst failing to make an appearance in 2017 for the Tigers, conducted themselves in the highest order whilst at the club. Fitzsimmons spent all of the season on-loan at Workington Town where he racked up an impressive 22 appearances, scoring two tries. Million meanwhile spent the season training with the first-team squad but failed to break through into the first team with Paul McShane having a stellar season at hooker.

French international, Kevin Larroyer came to the club in February of 2017 after being released by Hull KR following their relegation from Super League. He immediately went on loan to Bradford Bulls, for whom he played nine times, before making his Castleford debut in the away thrashing of Leigh. Kevin made seven appearances for the Tigers in total, but failed to score a try and has since joined Leigh Centurions for 2018.

Rugby League veteran Joel Monaghan linked up with the Tigers ahead of the 2016 season from Warrington Wolves where he averaged just over a try a game. He played 18 times in 2016 and 17 in 2017, scoring five tries in his first year at the club and eight in his second. Although his pace has somewhat deserted him, Joel still has a lot to offer any new suiter in terms of his experience and knowledge of the game.

Castleford born-and-bred Tom Holmes has been at the club since the tender age of 14. In 2016 Tom made seven appearances after debuting the year before. In 2017 Tom featured 12 times, scoring two tries and impressing with his cool head despite still only being 21. It was announced a week before the awards ceremony that he would be joining Featherstone Rovers on a one-year deal, despite interest from another Super League club and being contracted to the Tigers for 2018.

#29 - Luke Million

Luke joined the Tigers under 19s squad in 2014 from Huddersfield Giants' Scholarship programme and has been a key part of the Castleford Academy team since then. Unfortunately for Luke, he failed to make a single appearance for the Tigers' first-team despite impressing in the 2016 Boxing Day fixture against Hull FC and in the January

Date of Birth: 01/12/1997
Height: 189cm (5 ft 8)
Weight: 89kg (14 stone)
Country: England
Position: Hooker
Previous Clubs: Huddersfield Giants

friendly against Wakefield Trinity in which he scored a well-taken try from dummy half. It was also announced at Castleford's awards ceremony in September that Luke would be leaving the club at the end of the 2017 season. Perhaps if the Tigers had not been so hot on the field and if the team had been plagued with injuries, Castleford fans may well have seen Luke occupy a first-team spot. Luke does, however, leave the club with the well-wishes of all Tigers fans, some of whom were extremely disappointed to not actually see him on the field.

@TonyHarber - 26th December 2017: "Another try for Cas, Egodo finished great move after speedy break by Million and pass by McLelland. No goal - 36-0 #tigers"

@CTRLFC - 15th January 2017: "41: TRY CAS!!! Luke Million throws an outrageous dummy and dives over for the first score **of the second half. Trinity 4-28 Tigers"**

@CTRLFC - 15th January 2017: "FT: Trinity 32-30 Tigers. Luke Million scores the only try for Cas in the second half as a lot of youngsters earned valuable game time"

THE TRUEMAN SHOW!: TEENAGER STEALS THE SHOW IN ABSENCE OF GALE

With Luke Gale hospitalised on the Tuesday and with Ben Roberts still suffering from the knock he sustained against Leeds, Castleford ran with the unorthodox half-back pairing of Paul McShane and 18-year-old Jake Trueman. The latter was making his first start in a Tigers shirt having played a five-minute cameo against St Helens in June, and just two weeks after he had played in the academy Grand Final on the same ground.

In the week leading up to the game, Powell reiterated his intention to maintain the Tigers' momentum going into the play-off semi-final and he could not have been more pleased with the manner of his players' victory. Greg Eden, scoring his 38th try in the league, opened the scoring in the fifth minute after Trueman had timed a kick to perfection on a free play. The teenage sensation scored himself ten minutes later after latching onto a neat grubber by Adam Milner, playing at hooker for the first time since March's drubbing of the Rhinos. McShane failed with his first conversion but succeeded with the second and the Tigers were up 10-0 within 15 minutes.

Trueman then registered his second on 23 minutes and his third on 32 minutes, both fine individual scores that bewildered the hosts' defence, to notch up a remarkable 17-minute hat-trick that had the Tigers' fans, and most of Twitter, in sheer awe at such a wonderful first-half performance. With McShane kicking only one of the two further conversion attempts, the Tigers took a 20-0 lead going into the break. Passions had been running at a premium during the first forty and referee Ben Thaler twice instructed the team captains to calm their players whilst Tony Clubb had been placed on report for a late tackle on forward Nathan Massey which forced the latter to leave the field.

The Castleford onslaught continued after the break and the visitors extended their lead just five minutes in when Greg Minikin touched down in the corner after a superb offload from the rampaging Jake Webster. McShane added the extras and the Tigers were seemingly out of sight.

The hosts, however, clawed their way back into the game, scoring three tries in nine minutes. The first was a spectacular finish in the corner by winger Tom Davies on 52 minutes, followed by a Sam Tomkins effort three minutes later after he won the race to George Williams' kick. Wigan were well and truly back in it on the hour mark when Tommy Leuluai scampered over. With Williams converting two out of three, the visitors' lead had been cut to a mere 10 points

with just under 20 minutes remaining.

The Warriors desperately tried to find another try with both Joel Tomkins and Clubb being held up over the line by desperate Castleford defending. The sucker punch finally came with 11 minutes remaining as Tigers skipper Michael Shenton danced through some poor Wigan tackling for a fine solo score. Willie Isa did add some respectability to the scoreboard for the hosts with four minutes left, but the Tigers had the last laugh as Greg Minikin pounced on a Zak Hardaker kick as the full-time siren was about to go.

Before the game, the Warriors' play-off destiny was in their own hands. The Tigers, however, looked like the team desperate to earn a top-four spot. This hard-earned and well-deserved victory was also Castleford's fourth in a row over Wigan and the ease with which the Warriors were dispatched suggested it would not be their last. The absence of Gale had wafted in a sense of gloom amongst many Tigers fans. The introduction of Jake Trueman had all-but restored the hopeful optimism that this Castleford team could do something special.

WHAT THE FANS SAID

@MikePreston92: "Jake Trueman… remember the name!"

@free_oakers84: "Funny how people are saying Rugby League on its way out! Not in Cas what a team and season #SirDaryl."

@ClarksonSte: "When you lose both your starting half backs, only a True-Man stands up! #COYF."

@ianhenshaw1983: "Cracking result for @CTRLFC maybe Wigan should take note and leave the talking for on the field #LeagueLeaders #coyf."

@emmarshy: "Wow! Honestly thought we'd play it safe and save it all for the semi now. Love this team #COYF #slwigcas #castigers #rugbyleague."

LUKE GALE AND ZAK HARDAKER SHORTLISTED FOR MAN OF STEEL

Runaway leaders of the Betfred Super League, Castleford Tigers, dominated the three-man shortlist for 2017's Steve Prescott Man of Steel award. Chosen by a poll of every Super League player and presented to the individual deemed to have had the biggest impact on their team and the season as a whole, Castleford's Luke Gale and Zak Hardaker were joined by Hull FC stand-off Albert Kelly in the race to lift the most prestigious individual prize in the European game.

Gale has been in the form of his life in 2017, scoring over 300 points for Castleford, smashing his own record for the most points in a season in a Castleford jersey as well as retaining his place in the England squad which saw him feature in the May Test against Samoa. Integral to Castleford's pursuit of a place in the Grand Final, Gale proved himself to be one of the most consistent players in the Super League, steering the Tigers around the field and being majorly responsible for the way in which Castleford often easily dispatched their Super League rivals.

Joining Gale is team-mate and 2015 Man of Steel, Zak Hardaker. Originally signing with the Tigers on loan from Leeds Rhinos in November 2016, Hardaker filled the gaping hole left by Luke Dorn and quickly slotted into Daryl Powell's team. Zak seamlessly linked up with Castleford's attacking back line and was key to the Tigers scoring over 170 points in their opening four games as well as Castleford's remarkable achievement of ending the regular season scoring over 200 points more than their nearest competitors, Leeds Rhinos. After signing a permanent deal in June of 2017, Zak restored himself as the best full-back in the competition, rejuvenating himself on the field. Zak went on to play a pivotal role in Castleford's devastating attack, cementing a place in the top ten players for try assists. The season did of course end on

a tremendously sour note for Zak with his extradition from Castleford and England's squad due to a drugs infringement.

Whilst Castleford could well have had three nominees for the award (Greg Eden and Grant Millington to name but two), Hull FC half-back Albert Kelly did have a stellar season. After two years of playing on the east side of the city for Hull Kingston Rovers, Kelly swapped the red and white for the black and white of Hull FC in 2017 and never looked back. The former Hull KR talisman improved even further in 2017 and scooped four awards at the Hull FC's Player of the Year awards. At the time the shortlist was announced, Kelly was the club's top try-scorer and had formed a formidable partnership with fellow playmaker Marc Sneyd. The duo guided the team to a second successive Challenge Cup success as well as a top-four position in the Super 8s, however, Hull didn't manage to reach the Grand Final, losing out to Leeds Rhinos at Headingley.

The Steve Prescott Man of Steel results would be made public after the event was hosted in Manchester on Tuesday, October 3. It was not just the Man of Steel that would be awarded though as the evening also featured several other awards including Coach of the Year, Club of the Year, Foundation of the Year and Young Player of the Year. Nominees for the 2017 Betfred Super League Young Player of the Year were St Helens duo Morgan Knowles and Regan Grace and Wigan Warriors centre Oliver Gildart. Players must be under 21 years of age at the start of the season to be considered for the Young Player of the Year award.

GARRY LO SIGNS FOR THE TIGERS ON A TWO-YEAR DEAL WITH THE OPTION OF A THIRD

Garry Lo, a Papua New Guinean international, had been a revelation for Sheffield Eagles since he joined in 2016. Before moving to England Garry had been a firm fans favourite at Queensland Cup and second-tier side, PNG Hunters, where he scored 24 tries in 21 games and won the top try scorer award in the Hunters' inaugural season in 2014.

His record for Sheffield has been just as remarkable: 45 tries in 44 games. With a blockbusting running game and an ability to punch serious holes through the opponents defence, Garry is truly an exciting prospect who can have Castleford fans on their feet in 2018. Despite his small stature and powerful physique (just 5 ft 7, yet over 15 stones), Garry has an unbelievable leap and turn of pace that belies his size. Garry is more than capable of making the step up into Super League and has the potential to be yet another gem unearthed by Daryl Powell and his coaching staff.

Upon signing for the Tigers, Garry expressed his shock at being offered this chance in Super League, but also his determination to be a big hit: "I'm speechless! To be given this opportunity is a dream come true for me. To get the chance to test myself at the highest level in Super League is so exciting and I can't wait to join the boys soon for pre-season training."

Powell also spoke of his admiration for the way Garry plays the game and how well he can fit into the already star-ridden Castleford team: "Garry Lo has been a really exciting player for Sheffield over the last two years. I've had a good look at him and I think he will fit perfectly into the way that we play. He's an exciting player, he's very robust and a strong ball carrier who's got an ability to pass the ball as well, so I think he'll be a very exciting player to add into what we have already got."

Chief Executive Steve Gill added: "Garry is an excellent prospect, and at 23-years-old he is at a perfect age to move up into Super League from the Championship. I believe in time he will become a fans favourite, and Garry gives us real strength in depth on our wings."

The deal also included an agreement that Garry could be loaned back to Sheffield if/when he was not in the Castleford team.

#30 - Declan Sheehan

Declan started his rugby life with Dewsbury Moor before being scouted by Huddersfield Giants to join their scholarship scheme. He made the switch to Castleford at the end of 2014 and has progressed and impressed ever since in the Tigers under 19s set-up.

Date of Birth: 25/01/1998
Height: 183cm (6 ft)
Weight: 82kg (12.9 stone)
Country: England
Position: Wing
Previous Clubs: Huddersfield Giants

In 2017, Declan made the journey to full-time training with the first-team squad and has been widely tipped for a bright future. Declan did, however, find opportunities incredibly difficult to come by in 2017 with the likes of Greg Minkin, Greg Eden, Jy Hitchcox, Kieran Gill and Joel Monaghan all fighting for a wing spot.

In 2018, Declan may well be able to display his impressive speed and his eye for the try-line that made him such a valued member of the under 19s squad. However, it is perhaps more likely that Declan will go out on loan, much like Tuoyo Egodo and Will Maher, to build up that essential understanding of the rigours of first-team Rugby League.

@CTRLFC - 27th January 2017: "36: TRY CAS!! Dec Sheehan crosses in the corner after juggling with the final pass. Bulldogs 20-10 Tigers"

@WiganWarriorsRL - 8th April 2017: "28' TRY! Castleford pull one back with Declan Sheehan finishing acrobatically in the corner. Calum Turner fails to convert. CAS 4 WIG 12"

UNDERSTRENGTH TIGERS BEATEN BY TOP-FOUR CHASING HULL FC DESPITE DEBUTANT HAT-TRICK

With a semi-final just around the corner, in fact, in a mere six days, coach Daryl Powell took the option of resting several of his key men. Skipper Michael Shenton, workhorse Grant Millington, fullback Zak Hardaker and forwards Nathan Massey and Adam Milner were all rested, though Ben Roberts did return on the bench, with a view to keeping the squad as fresh as possible for the crunch clash against St Helens on the following Thursday.

Taking into consideration that Luke Gale, still sidelined after his appendix operation and still a doubt for the semi-final, and Junior Moors were still absent whilst Jake Trueman partnered Tom Holmes in the halves against the formidable duo of Albert Kelly and Marc Sneyd, the Tigers were in for a rough ride before the game had even begun.

Torrential rain allowed the visitors to do what they do best, pull the Tigers into a forward battle. The home side could not have started much worse, succumbing to a 10-0 deficit within 11 minutes as Albert Kelly and Jake Connor both scored when the hosts failed to deal with high kicks. Danny Houghton would also prosper from a similar outcome on 25 minutes. With two Sneyd conversions, Castleford already looked to be on the end of a battering.

Debutant Tuoyo Egodo, who showed up well on a tough night for the home side, then scored his first 11 minutes before the break when set up by a trademark Castleford move. But the Airlie Birds completed the first-half scoring with two tries in five minutes. First, Jamie Shaul took advantage of some soft defending to saunter through the Tigers' line and fool the Tigers fullback for the night, Greg Eden, on 34 minutes. And a minute before the hooter, Connor got his second, though referee Ben Thaler for some reason referred the decision to the video referee despite being in the best position possible. 28-6 to the visitors at the break, Castleford looked defeated as they trudged off the field.

However, whatever Powell had said at half-time certainly worked as Egodo registered two tries in four minutes just after the break to bring up a remarkable debut hat-trick, a similar feat to the week previous following Trueman's at Wigan on his first start for the club. This brought the Tigers back within 12 points.

Any thoughts of a comeback were wiped out on 52 minutes however as Connor also notched up his third of the night, exploiting weak defence once more. Sneyd slotted over a penalty ten minutes later to make it 16-36 which meant the Tigers would have to score four times. Carlos Tuimavave made the result beyond doubt on 64 minutes and the scoring was completed in the 70th minute as Jamie Shaul exploited some disappointing defence to skip through at least three tackles and send FC into a semi-final clash with Leeds Rhinos on the 29th. All-in-all, it was a truly dissatisfactory performance.

But with the list of absentees and the youthful and mismatched side Powell had put out, it was probably a result waiting to happen. This game just needed to be erased from the players' memory before the highly-anticipated semi-final just six days later. Yes, it was awful to watch, conceding eight tries and over forty points for the first time since last September, but it took no gloss off the remarkable achievements of the Tigers in 2017.

Castleford still had the League Leaders' Shield in their locker, the knowledge that they had broken Bradford's record of the number of points separating first and second in the league and, most importantly, their well-deserved semi-final place. All focus was now aimed at beating St Helens and securing a Grand Final spot. The atmosphere at the Mend-a-Hose Jungle promised to be one of the best in Rugby League history. Could Castleford achieve what just a few years ago, seemed downright impossible?

WHAT THE FANS SAID

@swanseagas: "Think we could regret not taking the opportunity to push Hull out of the top 4. Only team I fear in the knockout stages…#coyf."

@LaurenciumSmith: "Disappointing loss tonight for @CTRLFC but in Daryl we trust! Onwards and upwards for next week's semi-final #COYF."

@BlokeFromCas: "OK, ladies and gentlemen. Forget this ever happened, crack on in training and start afresh on Thursday. #COYF."

@underwood_81: "I really hope this doesn't have a negative impact on the squad for next week. It's been an awful performance. #COYF."

@WaltonTiger: "I know it wasn't, but tonight's game felt something to get through. Win together, lose together. Rock the lane next week together! #COYF."

SIX CASTLEFORD PLAYERS INCLUDED IN THE 2017 BETFRED SUPER LEAGUE DREAM TEAM

Castleford Tigers' dominance throughout the Super League in 2017 was reflected in the number of players selected as the best in their position for that season. Greg Eden, Luke Gale, Zak Hardaker, Mike McMeeken, Grant Millington and Michael Shenton all made up part of the Dream Team, which is voted for by the sport's broadcasters and journalists in a secret ballot.

Six other Super League clubs were also represented, but none amassed a number even close to the six sported by table-toppers Castleford. Hull FC were represented by two players, whilst Huddersfield Giants, St Helens, Leeds Rhinos, Salford Red Devils and Wigan Warriors all had one of their players included.

The 2017 Dream Team also featured eight debut players, including Eden, McMeeken and Millington alongside Huddersfield Giants' Sebastine Ikahihifo, St Helens' centre Mark Percival and Leeds Rhinos hooker Matt Parcell. Wigan Warriors and England Captain Sean O'Loughlin notched up a remarkable sixth Dream Team appearance, three years since his last appearance in 2014. The three other Castleford representatives, Hardaker, Gale and Shenton, made their third Dream Team appearances.

The 2017 Betfred Super League Dream Team was as follows (order of their positions on the field):

Zak Hardaker (*Castleford Tigers*) Dream Team appearances: 3 (*2014, 2015, 2017*)

Greg Eden (*Castleford Tigers*) Dream Team appearances: 1 (*2017*)
Michael Shenton (*Castleford Tigers*) Dream Team appearances: 3 (*2014, 2015, 2017*)
Mark Percival (*St Helens*) Dream Team appearances: 1 (*2017*)
Mahe Fonua (*Hull FC*) Dream Team appearances: 2 (*2016, 2017*)
Albert Kelly (*Hull FC*) Dream Team appearances: 1 (*2017*)
Luke Gale (*Castleford Tigers*) Dream Team appearances: 3 (*2015, 2016, 2017*)
Grant Millington (*Castleford Tigers*) Dream Team appearances: 1 (*2017*)
Matt Parcell (*Leeds Rhinos*) Dream Team appearances: 1 (*2017*)
Sebastine Ikahihifo (*Huddersfield Giants*) Dream Team appearances: 1 (*2017*)
Ben Murdoch-Masila (*Salford Red Devils*) Dream Team appearances: 1 (*2017*)
Mike McMeeken (*Castleford Tigers*) Dream Team appearances: 1 (*2017*)
Sean O'Loughlin (*Wigan Warriors*) Dream Team appearances: 6 (*2010, 2011, 2012, 2013, 2014, 2017*)

Although Castleford had six players included, it could well have been seven. Paul McShane must have been close to registering his first Dream Team appearance after a superb season with the Tigers. He would almost certainly have been included had Parcell not had such a stellar year in his first season in England with the Rhinos.

LUKE GALE NAMED THE RUGBY LEAGUE WRITERS' PLAYER OF THE YEAR

The celebration of Luke Gale's season was simply unstoppable; to add to his third successive Albert Goldthorpe Medal, his inclusion in the 2017 Dream Team, being shortlisted for the Man of Steel award and the breaking of two records for Castleford Tigers (for the number of conversions in a season and number of points in a season), Luke was also named the Rugby League Writers and Broadcasters Association's Player of the Year.

Luke beat off competition from Wigan Warriors' Sean O'Loughlin as well as his teammates, Greg Eden, Zak Hardaker, Paul McShane and Grant Millington to scoop the Raymond Fletcher Memorial Trophy. He would be presented with the trophy and a replica at the turn of 2018. The trophy is named after the late Raymond Fletcher who was the sport's official statistician from 1991 until his retirement in 2011 as well as the Yorkshire Post Rugby League correspondent from 1975 until 1995.

#31 - Brandon Westerman

Brandon joined Castleford in 2014 after playing for his local side, Castleford Panthers. He soon impressed in the under19s setup and began training with the Tigers' first-team in 2015. Although he failed to register a first-team appearance, he inked a new deal in May

Date of Birth: 26/02/1997
Height: 183cm (6 ft)
Weight: 93kg (14.9 stone)
Country: England
Position: Second-Row

2015 which would have seen him at the club until the end of 2017. Given squad number 31 at the clubs' 2017 pre-season launch and with the potential to rival his cousin and former Tigers' player Joe, Brandon could well have fought for a place on the field if he had truly wanted to

However, with just one Boxing Day appearance in the home thrashing of Hull FC, Brandon requested a release from his contract midway through January 2017. Brandon failed to attract any new suiters and it wasn't until March that he was given a trial by Hull FC and assigned to their Reserves team, where he put in a few good performances. In July, he was again on the move, this time on loan to Doncaster until the end of the season. It is a shame that Brandon was never able to force his way into Daryl Powell's plans as he is a talented player with a physical edge that could well have adapted to the Castleford style of play in 2017.

@hullfcfanzine - 11th March 2017: "Debut try for Brandon Westerman. Great hands from Wray and the back rower finishes superbly. Rawsthorne converts. 44-24. "

@LewScott97 - 21st July 2017: "Hull FC send Ross Osborne on loan to York, while Nick Rawsthorne, Brandon Westerman and Hakim Maloudi join Doncaster. #RLTransferDeadlineDay"

PULSATING ENCOUNTER SEES SAINTS DENIED IN EXTRA TIME AS CASTLEFORD MAKE YET MORE HISTORY

In what can arguably be described as the best play-off semi-final in Super League history, Castleford Tigers snatched victory from the jaws of defeat against a St Helens side that had led with just one minute to go.

All the talk before the game, in the media and amongst fans, focused on whether or not Luke Gale would play. After having an appendix operation just 16 days prior to the biggest Castleford match in the Super League era, Luke took to the field in an almost Lazarus-like effort. Half a kilo lighter and with doctors giving him a three-week rest period, the decision, made by Luke himself, seemed a risky one. But it was a decision that will go down in Castleford history as one of the best ever made by a player. A 15-point haul, including a last-minute penalty to even the game up when the Tigers seemed dead and buried and a well-taken extra-time drop-goal to bring the victory home, firmly etched Luke's name into Castleford folklore.

The atmosphere at the Mend-a-Hose Jungle was tense with anticipation before referee James Child blew the first whistle at 7:45 pm. The anxiety in the air was wiped out within the opening minute as a Saints knock-on from a towering Zak Hardaker kick-off gave the hosts vital early field position. And from the resulting scrum, a neat Gale one-two with Jesse Sene-Lefao opened up a huge gap in the visitors' defence. Gale then fed Hardaker with precision, after a tremendous lead-run by captain Michael Shenton, and Hardaker had the footwork and strength to skip over to give the Tigers a dream start. Gale converted and added a penalty on eight minutes to send the home side into an 8-0 lead before Saints had taken the ball into the Tigers' half.

It took 16 minutes for the visitors to register their first points of the night when Regan Grace finished acrobatically in the corner after great work by impressive full-back Ben Barba. With Mark Percival unsuccessful with the conversion, it was 8-4 to the Tigers.

Greg Minikin thought he had scored for Castleford after Percival dropped a high kick, but was adjudged to have knocked-on in the act of scoring. And aided by five successive penalties, the visitors ended the half on top following a neat planned move which saw Morgan Knowles crash over from a James Roby pass on 37 minutes. Percival would add the extras for the first and only time, a statistic that came back to haunt him and St Helens, and the visitors led 10-8 at half-time.

In the second half, the game ebbed and flowed dramatically with little to no involvement by the referee as both sides played their part in a magnificent forty minutes of rugby.

Defence was of the highest order from both sides and only Paul McShane's desperate tackle on James Roby held the visitors out, whilst the valiant Saints defence was finally breached 17 minutes into the second half. Luke Gale fired the ball towards Greg Eden who side-stepped Makinson with pure skill, before sprinting down the wing with Gale on hand to take the return pass. And with the half-back's conversion, the hosts were back into the lead once more at 14-10. In celebrating his try, Gale lifted his shirt up to reveal the bandage around his stomach, a by-product of his appendix operation, and in doing so, demonstrated his true warrior-like determination to even be on the field.

Castleford began turning the screw and after being under the cosh for most of the game, extended the lead to 20-10 on 64 minutes when Adam Milner, after he himself had performed an astonishing last-ditch tackle on Makinson to haul him in to touch with the try-line open, forced his way over from close range for another converted try.

There is a term in Rugby League that states "don't write off the Saints", and the final ten minutes displayed why. The visitors, looking down and out after Milner's effort, responded on 70 minutes as Makinson finished strongly after more good work by Barba. Then, just three minutes later, Percival hit a great line from another Barba pass to crash over. With the try-scorer, Percival's, two missed conversions, the visitors were still behind at 20-18.

The comeback was complete, however, when an off-the-cuff last-tackle move saw James Roby storm down the middle of the Tigers' defence after receiving an Alex Walmsley offload. Roby, with the presence of mind to head for the right-hand corner, sent out a

huge pass to centre Ryan Morgan who had the pace to beat the covering defence. With just two minutes on the clock, the Saints' players, officials and fans were in raptures, believing they had won a frenetic encounter. Another Percival missed kick though left the home side just two points behind.

The Castleford players had been on their haunches with their heads in their hands after Morgan's score, yet rallied to the half-way line for one last gigantic push with a minute left. Hardaker's brilliant short kick-off saw the Tigers regather the ball. And, with literally seconds on the clock, a kick through by Gale was recovered with ease by the Saints' defence. The touch judge, however, had noticed an infringement on Shenton as the kick went through and referee Child made the bold, but correct, decision to award the Tigers a penalty on the hooter.

Gale boldly stepped up and dispatched the kick with ease, sending the match into extra-time with golden-point deciding the winner. As he did so, the atmosphere around the packed-out Jungle became even more nerve-wracking.

The Castleford pack had been out on their feet in the last ten minutes of normal time, yet they found the energy from somewhere to restrict Saints' go-forward and ensure Matty Smith was 40 yards out when he took a speculative drop-goal attempt after Gale had too failed with a one-pointer. Back came the home side. With a formidable drive by the recently-returned Junior Moors, the Tigers were in good field position.

As McShane attempted to eke a penalty from James Child, Moors now stepped into dummy-half. With a well-executed pass and forwards Grant Millington and Adam Milner getting poleaxed for their protection of Gale, the scrum-half delivered a drop-goal in the 88th minute that sent the Castleford fans into absolute delirium.

It was a heart-wrenching end for the Saints, who despite finishing the season 17 points behind the Tigers, played their part in an emotionally-charged, fast-paced and intense battle and were the better team for much of the game.

For the Tigers, the tag of not being able to win big games had been well and truly discarded. And the jubilation of reaching their maiden Grand Final was there for all to see on the terraces and on the field as fans, who before the game had never spoken to each other, embraced each other as if they were family members, whilst the battle-weary players jumped on their half-back hero with pure glee.

2017 was like no other that Castleford fans had witnessed in the modern era: a League Leaders' Shield and now a Grand Final appearance had not just upset the traditional Super League order; it had completely destroyed it. Old Trafford beckoned for a team, club and town that ten years to the day before had competed in a Championship Grand Final for a place back amongst the elite and just three years before had been on the brink of administration. For Tigers fans, it was hard not to believe that 2017 was a dream and that one day they would wake up. But the moment their beloved team would walk out into the 'Theatre of Dreams', the Castleford fans would finally realise that it was in fact, a reality.

WHAT THE FANS SAID

@nick_raynor: "Last night was absolutely epic. Still keep watching the highlights over and over. What a game of rugby. @CTRLFC in the Grand Final! #COYF."

@Peacocks66: "Forget Alton Towers @CTRLFC last night's game was the best rollercoaster ride I have ever ridden…need a week off work to recover #COYF."

@jainecashart: "Got to admit stood & cried like a girl at the end! Not normally lost for words but I am tonight. Blood pressure must have been sky high #COYF."

@HantsCastiger: "To every @CTRLFC player – thank you for giving me the opportunity to see you all at Old Trafford next week. Never thought I'd see the day."

@deborah7newsome: "Wow just wow I love this club, what an amazing achievement. Old Trafford here we come @CTRLFC #coyf #SweetCaroline."

@Beachhyyy: "WOW. That has to be the most nail biting, thrilling, heart stopping game I've been to. That feeling was indescribable @CTLRFC #COYF."

OUTRAGEOUS OCTOBER

CASTLEFORD WIN BIG AT SUPER LEAGUE'S AWARDS NIGHT FOR 2017

Castleford Tigers celebrated their historic season in Manchester as they scooped up Club of the Year, with Greg Eden earning the Top Tryscorer Award and Daryl Powell and Luke Gale rightly receiving Coach of the Year and Man of Steel respectively.

Albert Goldthorpe Medal winner three years in a row, record points scorer for Castleford in a season, 2017 Dream Team member and Rugby League Writers' Player of the Year, Luke Gale had won just about every prize available in the 2017 season. He added yet another accolade to his impressive CV when he became 2017's Man of Steel.

In doing so, Gale became only the fourth Castleford player to win the prize, following in the footsteps of Adrian Vowles (1999), Rangi Chase (2011) and Daryl Clark (2014). Luke narrowly beat his teammate Zak Hardaker to the prize, securing just 32 more points than the former Leeds fullback with 481 points to Zak's 449. Hull FC's Albert Kelly finished third with 267 points and his Black-and-Whites teammate Mahe Fonua came in fourth with 158. Rather than being an outright voting system, players have three choices: first, second and third. Players' first placed choice received five points, second-placed three points and their third choice received one point.

With the Grand Final still to go, Gale had racked up 27 appearances for the Tigers in 2017, scoring 13 tries, with 20 try assists,

304 tackles and 141 carries. And even more spectacularly, he had made a miraculous recovery from appendix surgery just in time to help his teammates seal a dramatic Semi-Final win over St Helens and a Grand Final clash with local rivals Leeds Rhinos. An award chosen by their peers, to receive this prize is a player's greatest individual

accolade. Speaking on stage at the event in Manchester, Gale said: "I'm immensely proud to receive this great award, it's a great accolade to pick up! I've had a great journey in my career and especially this year, and it's not over yet."

Gale added: "I signed for Cas three years ago, I met Daryl Powell and I knew after that first meeting that I wanted to be part of this club. I knew what Daryl was building and I wanted to be part of it. All the boys just love the club, we love turning up for training, we love our jobs and that's down to the great environment Daryl has built. We just love being part of this great team."

Greg Eden was also presented with Super League's award for Top Tryscorer with 38 tries for the season up to this point. Eden was just two shy of Denny Solomona's record of 40 tries in the league in 2016 with one game to go. The flyer was, however, a massive 18 tries ahead of second-placed Albert Kelly.

Unsurprisingly, Daryl Powell was awarded the Coach of the Year after Castleford's brilliant season with seven votes, whilst Wakefield Trinity boss Chris Chester was second with five votes. Powell himself voted for Chester.

The Tigers were not finished there however and were lauded with the prize of being Club of the Year. Steve Gill, Castleford's heroic Chief Executive, collected the award and dedicated it to the late Jack Fulton, the kind-hearted former Chairman of the club, and his wife Bridie. It was also announced on the night that Castleford Tigers had increased their attendances for the regular season by 13% and in the Super 8s by a whopping 23%.

Wigan Warriors' centre Oliver Gildart picked up Young Player of the Year award after

playing a shining role in a disappointing season for the Lancashire club.

Castleford's Andy Lynch, retiring at the end of the season after 452 Super League games, was presented with an outstanding achievement in Super League award for making more than 200 appearances for the Tigers. Others who have retired, or who are set to retire, also received outstanding achievements awards. These included Leeds Rhinos' Rob Burrow, Huddersfield Giants' Earl Crabtree, Hull FC captain and stalwart Gareth Ellis, Doncaster's Iafeta Palea'aesina, ex-Bradford Bulls half-back Leon Pryce, Catalans' longest-serving player Thomas Bosc and Widnes's Chris Bridge.

The way in which Castleford swept the board at this awards night was reminiscent of how they had utterly dominated the Super League competition as a whole in 2017. There was just one game that stood between this group of players and the club and a truly remarkable, almost utopian season.

BEN CROOKS DEPARTS THE CLUB TO JOIN LEIGH CENTURIONS

Castleford Tigers confirmed that centre Ben Crooks had made his loan switch permanent to Lancashire club Leigh Centurions for a five-figure sum.

Ben made his Super League debut for Hull FC in 2012 after graduating through their academy ranks. In the following season, Ben earned a place in the 2013 Super League Dream Team after scoring 20 tries in 22 games as well as forming a prolific centre-wing partnership with Tom Lineham. The 2014 season did not run as smoothly for Ben and he signed for NRL side Parramatta Eels in September 2014.

Pontefract-born Crooks then joined the Tigers ahead of the 2016 season on a three-year deal. Although a first-team regular in 2016, scoring six tries in 28 appearances, Crooks spent the entirety of 2017 on loan at Leigh and had been one of their most consistent performers despite their relegation from Super League in the Million-Pound Game. Still only 24 years of age, Crooks scored six tries in 23 games for the Centurions in 2017.

With little chance of Ben forcing his way back into the Castleford side for 2018 following the signing of Joe Wardle as well as the impressive performances of centres Jake Webster and Michael Shenton in 2017, coach Daryl Powell understandably allowed Ben to link up permanently with Leigh.

Powell stated: "Ben has spent the entire 2017 season with Leigh Centurions and has been one of their outstanding players across the whole season. We are well covered in the centre and outside backs and we believe that it is in the best interest of both Ben and ourselves that he should stay with Leigh for the coming season. I would like to thank Ben for all his hard work whilst he was at the Tigers and I wish him all the best for the future."

Leigh owner Derek Beaumont waxed lyrical about Ben's commitment to his club following

their relegation and the standards he brought to the club: "Ben is a great bloke to have around your club and has really bought into the place. He has been a solid performer for us all year and will only get better as time goes on. His commitment to return from injury early to take part in the last few games speaks volumes for him.

Beaumont added: "The fact he was prepared to commit to the club in either competition is another clear demonstration that the club is driving forward and our relegation is a minor setback. It has been a real pleasure having Ben at the club and I look forward to seeing him back in a Leigh shirt next year."

Ben commented on how much he had enjoyed his time at Leigh: "While clouded by defeat in the Million Pound Game, I have thoroughly enjoyed the on and off field experience here at the Centurions. The longer-term ambitions of the club under owner Derek Beaumont are clearly stated and evident in current team recruitment for an immediate return to Super League."

Including a dual registration spell at Doncaster, Ben has scored 48 tries and kicked 31 goals in 105 senior games so far in his career.

All Castleford fans wish him all the best in his future endeavours and thank him for the role he played in the Tigers' 2016 season. It's a shame that he was unable to follow in his father's Lee Crooks's, who played more than 200 games for the Tigers over a period of eight years, footsteps and become a legend at the club.

#32 - Daniel Igbinedion

Date of Birth: 26/01/1995
Height: 187cm (6 ft 1)
Weight: 102kg (16.1 stone)
Country: England
Position: Prop/ Second-Row
Previous Clubs: London Broncos, Oxford RL, Dewsbury Rams (loan)

Daniel rose through the academy ranks at London Broncos before moving to Oxford at the end of 2015. The promising forward played 21 times for Oxford in the League 1 competition during 2016. His performances did not go unnoticed as he scooped the Most Improved Player award at the club's end of season awards. Daniel developed so well in his maiden season with Oxford that he caught the eye of the Tigers coaching staff. Daniel was invited by Tigers head coach Daryl Powell to spend a week in the full-time environment following positive reports by Oxford's head coach Tim Rumford, where he impressed enough to earn a two-year deal in October 2016.

'Iggy', as he is known to his friends, played in three of Castleford's four pre-season friendlies where he generally impressed with his strong running and physical defence. With first-team places limited, Daniel went on loan to Dewsbury Rams for much-needed game time, appearing 15 times and scoring one try and delivering two man-of-the-match performances in the process.

Daniel still could not crack the first-team and left the club permanently on the 29th June 2017 after failing to make an appearance. Local rivals Featherstone Rovers snapped up the powerful forward and he went on to make three substitute appearances for the club. It was a shame that Daniel never got to show the Castleford fans whether or not he was cut out for Super League.

After bright performances in the three friendlies, he did get to play in a Tigers' jersey, many fans were disappointed not to see him play in the regular season. Daniel did, however, move on with all of Castleford's best wishes and all would want to wish him good luck in the future.

@DewsburyRams - 4th June 2017: "31m- Nearly another try for the Rams as Igbinedion nearly makes it over the line. Score stays the same. Rams 10 Bulls 12"

@Halifax_RLFC - 7th May 2017: 22' TRY! The Rams take advantage of the error as Daniel Igbinedion powers over from Squires inside offload (4-6) #RAMvHAL

THE 'THEATRE OF NIGHTMARES': TIGERS DISAPPOINT WHEN IT MATTERS MOST

On a rain-drenched evening that typified the infamous Grand Final weather, Castleford ended their remarkable season with a performance that must rank as one of the worst ever to grace the Old Trafford turf. The Tigers made 18 errors: a Grand Final record; and ended the match with less than a 50% completion rate. These two statistics, compiled with the notorious absence of fullback sensation Zak Hardaker and the subsequent disruption, played into a Leeds team's hands whose two long-serving stars, Rob Burrow and Danny McGuire, were striving for a fairytale end to their illustrious Rhinos' careers. The week leading up to the end-of-season crunch clash had started positively for Castleford; enthusiasm and pride were rife amongst the fans. And why not? They were up against a team that they had beaten eight times in a row and four times in 2017. This was a Leeds team that was nothing special as Castleford had proved throughout the season. But, it was also a Leeds team filled with big-game experience and multiple Grand Final rings between them. For this reason alone, the Rhinos' fans were hopeful, yet nervous considering the recent hold their opponents had had over them.

When Thursday came along, this hope turned into belief as the Castleford 19-man squad was released. There was no Zak Hardaker. The ex-Leeds man was dropped from the team for 'a breach of club rules' that was later revealed to be the result of him failing of a drugs test taken after the Super 8s victory over Leeds Rhinos. It was a bitter blow for the Tigers whose attacking flair and defensive solidity in 2017 had owed lots to Zak's command and ability at the back.

Greg Eden had played the No.1 role previously at the Tigers in 2017 as well as his previous clubs. But he simply does not bring the same authority as Hardaker. With just one training session left before the 'big dance' on the Saturday, it was an omission that affected Castleford greatly, both on the field and in the terraces.

Fans, who up until the Thursday had been sick with excitement, now began to doubt and question why Zak had been left out a mere two days before the most important game in Castleford's history. Greg Eden, whose masterful season haul of 38 tries as a winger had been one of many highlights of the Castleford season, found himself at fullback with Jy

Hitchcox coming in on the wing. But all three of Castleford's back men, Eden, Hitchcox and Minikin, looked like rabbits caught in headlights as Leeds incessantly peppered all three with towering bombs.

The way Castleford had lit up the Super League in 2017 had been nothing short of stunning. Yet the way in which the Tigers' season ended with their worst performance for a couple of years will be the lingering, painful memory that many Castleford fans will take away from such a stellar year overall.

The torrential rain before and during the kick-off on yet another gloomy Manchester evening did not help proceedings. Known for their expansive and inventive play, the Tigers could not get into their stride. And in the difficult conditions, it was a surprise that the Tigers passed up the opportunity to take three very kickable penalties that would have given Castleford the confidence to kick on and produce the magic that the Rugby League world know they could.

The first rejection of two points proved costly when Tom Briscoe, who just a few months ago had looked bereft of confidence, leapt above Jy Hitchcox to take a Danny McGuire kick to the corner in the 11th minute. Kallum Watkins' conversion made it 6-0.

Watkins himself thought he had Leeds' second just six minutes later when he won the race to a McGuire grubber only to be denied by video referee Phil Bentham, who was called upon regularly by referee James Child, for a knock-on.

With the Tigers gradually feeling their way into the game, they ran another penalty deep inside the Rhinos' half, but Eden knocked on with the try line begging. Moments later, prop Grant Millington rampaged his way close to the line, but was brought back for a forward pass by referee Child, who it must be said, had a composed game in what was his first Grand Final appointment.

Jy Hitchcox then believed he had scored from a Luke Gale kick through only for Bentham to rule that Oliver Holmes had obstructed the defence despite him not affecting the play.

Leeds once more went down to the Castleford end and Briscoe looked to have scored his second only for Bentham to again rule no try for a push in McShane's back.

It was a dismal first-half with little to shout about for either team with the only remaining point of the opening forty coming from the boot of McGuire as he added a drop-goal just before the hooter. 7-0 down at half-time was not impossible to overcome. But the Tigers somehow dished up an even more incompetent display in the second forty to hand the game on a plate to Leeds.

Castleford continued to invite unwarranted pressure on their line through abysmal ball retention and lack of communication. And on 52 minutes, Leeds made this pressure tell when Joel Moon's high kick was spilt by Eden into the grateful arms of McGuire. Watkins failed to convert, but on the hour mark Leeds turned the screw as Moon created something out of nothing to feed Briscoe, albeit with a forward pass, to cross in the corner. With Watkins' second successful conversion of the night, the Tigers were now 17-0 down.

McGuire then put the result beyond doubt in the 72nd minute after a Leeds kick had been lost yet again by the Tigers' covering defence. Castleford did look to have scored a consolation try minutes later as Eden went over following smart work by Hitchcox, but the latter was ruled to have put a foot in touch by video referee Bentham.

Adding salt into the wounds as Luke Gale had done twice to the Rhinos in 2017, McGuire added a drop goal with three minutes left to make it 24-0.

Castleford's blushes for being the only team to be nilled in a Grand Final were spared when Alex Foster, who just eight months ago had been without a job and at risk of exiting the game, pounced on a McShane kick after the Tigers had thrown caution to the wind with just a minute left. Gale converted as the hooter sounded, but there was nothing to celebrate. The best team by far in 2017 had come up short against a team who had 42 Grand Final rings between them and who had now won their eighth Super League title.

Too many errors, a lack of playing the conditions, team disruption and being up against a Leeds team determined to send off two of their greatest Super League players with another title under their belt, the Tigers just could not get going. This was replicated in the stands as the atmosphere in the Stretford End fell flat midway through the first half as the Castleford supporters began to realise it was just not their team's day. The fans needed something to cheer, unfortunately, this only came in the 79th minute and when the game was already dead and buried.

The Tigers undoubtedly saved their worst performance of the season for when it mattered most. However, this should not take the shine off how far Castleford had come in 2017. League leaders for the first time in 91 years, hailed as the Club of the Year with both the Coach of the Year and Man of Steel in their ranks with six Dream Team players and above all a well-deserved Grand Final appearance, 2017 was truly a breakthrough year for the Tigers in all sense of the word. It is such a shame that the Tigers fell far short of the expectations that the club, the fans and neutrals watching around the world, expected to see on the 7th of October.

WHAT THE FANS SAID

@LJ_YH2: "Very very proud to be a Cas fan this year! Still hurting and upset but looking back it's been a great year! Can't wait for 2018 #COYF."

@PaulBailes11: "@CTRLFC We'll be back. We're an awesome club with the best fans in the league #futuresbright #COYF."

@WWWoodzy92: "Tough one to take but this team will go places and no doubt next season we will be thereabouts once again! Rollercoaster year #COYF."

@MrLeeArmitage: "Shame about the result but sure we will be back stronger and better for it. It's been a fantastic season. More to come! #COYF."

@TomCottam6: "Yesterday's disappointment gives us today's motivation. Recover your bodies and minds because the hard work will soon begin. #COYF."

@nogis: "It has been an amazing season and thank you @CTRLFC for the most amazing journey. 2017 must go down as one of the best seasons ever. #COYF."

#33 - Kevin Larroyer

Date of Birth: 19/06/1989
Height: 185cm (6 ft 1)
Weight: 96kg (15.1 stone)
Country: France
Position: Second Row
Previous Clubs: Toulouse Olympique, Catalans Dragons, Hull KR, Bradford Bulls (loan)
National Honours: 14 Caps for France

Appearances: 7	**Avg. Gain:** 6.74
Tries: 0	**Tackles:** 121
Try Assists: 2	**Clean Breaks:** 0
Metres: 310	**Offloads:** 1

Kevin started his career with Toulouse before moving to Catalans Dragons in 2012. In 2013, he went on loan to Hull KR for the entire season and signed a permanent deal with them the following year. But upon KR's relegation from Super League in 2016, Kevin was told he was surplus to requirements, despite being part way through a three-year deal.

Frantically searching for a club for 2017, he was allowed to train with Hull FC, but they made it clear there was no salary cap space to take Kevin on a contract. As such, the Tigers stepped in, and as of the 15th February, he was a Castleford player until the end of 2017 with a two-year option beyond that. He immediately went on loan to Bradford Bulls for much-needed game time where he made nine appearances.

His debut for the Tigers came in the away thrashing of Leigh in late April where he appeared comfortable and energetic despite lacking Super League match fitness. Kevin would make only six more appearances for Castleford and would be told the club would not take up their initial two-year extension option. The Frenchman was not afraid to do a shift in defence, helping his teammates out admirably with some big-hitting tackles and rarely was he found wanting in the line. It was also quite humbling to see Kevin take Gadwin Springer under his wing. With Kevin's arrival, Gadwin had someone who could help him interpret the game and increase his understanding of the English culture as Kevin had been in England since 2013.

Many Tigers fans were upset that Kevin would not be turning out for their club in 2018, with most feeling he had not been given a proper chance to showcase his credentials. But given the competitive nature of the Castleford squad, Kevin simply could not force his way into the team consistently. Kevin leaves the club with all of Castleford's best wishes.

@JackTJackson95 – 17th August 2017: "Just a bit of a thought for @KevinLarroyer – relegated and no contract a year ago. League Leaders winner (probably) tonight. Every cloud!"

@MattCore180 – 25th July 2017: "@Kevin Larroyer been a fine addition to the squad, given your all every game…keep it going mate.'

@PeterOsbornCas – 15th February 2017: "Happy with the signing of Kevin Larroyer, decent player that will add depth to the pack #COYF."

ZAK HARDAKER PROVISIONALLY SUSPENDED FOR USE OF A BANNED SUBSTANCE

In a club statement, Castleford Tigers confirmed that it had received notification that Zak Hardaker had tested positive for a banned substance following the Tigers' Super 8s match against Leeds Rhinos on 8th September 2017.

The club was made aware at 10:00 am on Thursday morning that the player would receive official written notification from UK Anti-Doping and therefore the player was immediately suspended. With Zak being removed from the 19-man squad for the Grand Final – which would be played just two days later - Castleford fans and the whole rugby league fraternity were in a frenzy, frantically trying to work out why he would be absent from the Tigers' most important Super League match in history after playing such a vital role for Castleford in 2017.

Official notification was delivered to the club on Friday and following discussions with the player on Sunday the decision was taken to announce the result of the test in order to clarify the circumstances around Zak's omission for the highly-anticipated Grand Final on the 7th.

Zak issued a sincere apology: "I would like to apologise to my Castleford Tigers teammates, the staff and all fans for my enormous error of judgment. I was given an opportunity by this great club and in what has been one of the most important weeks in its history, I have let everyone at the club down. For that, I truly apologise."

"Finally, I would like to make it clear that in no way did I, nor would I, ever take a substance with the intention of enhancing my performance."

A spokesperson for the governing body, the Rugby Football League, said: "The Rugby Football League can confirm that Zak Hardaker is provisionally suspended from all competition after it received notification from UK Anti-Doping that he had tested positive for a banned substance following a Super 8s game between Castleford Tigers and Leeds Rhinos on September 8, 2017.

"He will therefore not be considered for the England Rugby League World Cup squad due to be announced today (Monday) at 12 pm.

"The Rugby Football League will be making no further comment until the outcome of the case has been determined."

If the outcome of the case determined Zak to be guilty, he would face at least a two-year ban from the sport.

#34 - Alex Foster

Date of Birth: 25/09/1993
Height: 185cm (6 ft 1)
Weight: 96kg (15.1 stone)
Country: England
Position: Second Row
Previous Clubs: Leeds Rhinos, Hunslet (loan), London Broncos (loan), Featherstone Rovers (loan), Oxford RL (loan)

Appearances: 18	**Avg. Gain:** 6.72
Tries: 2	**Tackles:** 389
Try Assists: 0	**Clean Breaks:** 2
Metres: 874	**Offloads:** 6

Alex came through the Leeds Rhinos academy, making his Super League debut in 2013. Despite signing a three-year contract at the end of 2013 with Leeds, he spent 2014 and 2015 on loan at London Broncos and Featherstone Rovers respectively. In 2016 he moved back to London, this time permanently, on a two-year deal. But ahead of the 2017 season, he relocated north once more to Bradford Bulls, signing a two-year contract. Once the Bulls went into liquidation in January 2017 however, Alex became a free agent.

With a lack of attention from other clubs because of his injuries, Foster considered retiring to pursue other career avenues. Castleford however offered Alex hope. The Tigers brought Alex in on an initial trial basis in February 2017 with the view of signing a two-year contract and it was signed in June after he did enough to impress Powell despite his injury problems. This would prove to be one of Powell's most inspired decisions of 2017.

Since debuting for the Tigers at Huddersfield in May, Alex became a regular figure in the team, appearing 19 times and scoring twice. Ironically, his first try of the season came against his first club, Leeds, in September. When a high kick bounced into his arms, Alex shrugged off three defenders and stretched valiantly for the line. Alex's story truly hit the realms of fantasy when he became the first and only Castleford player to score in a Super League Grand Final. His defensive enthusiasm was obvious; he was regularly one of Castleford's top three tacklers, averaging around 30 per game and even accumulating a massive 44 tackles against Hull FC in September. His attacking play also improved drastically during 2017; towards the season's end, his link-up play with Luke Gale and his superb line-running was great to watch. Alex displayed all the qualities and attributes that make him a Super League player without question. Foster definitely has the talent to make that second row spot his own in 2018.

@B_Hammonds – 28th September 2017: "We sign Alex Foster to play Championship Rugby, doesn't play for us moves to Cas and helped them to a GF. We did miss out there massively."
@Gerbelly – 7th October 2017: "Easy to miss Alex Foster's story. Was originally gonna be playing Championship for Bulls in 2017. Made redundant, now playing in Grand Final."
@CallumLand – 3rd August 2017: "What a find this guy has been, he's took his chance and then some."

LUKE GALE AND MIKE MCMEEKEN MAKE 24-MAN SQUAD FOR ENGLAND AHEAD OF WORLD CUP

Castleford Tigers players Luke Gale and Mike McMeeken will both be representing England in November at the World Cup after being chosen by coach Wayne Bennett following outstanding seasons from the duo.

Mike McMeeken was excited about representing his country: "It's a massive honour to have been selected for the World Cup squad. I'm looking forward to getting the opportunity to represent my country again on an international stage"

Luke Gale could not hide his enthusiasm at participating in the World Cup experience: "It's a huge honour to have been selected to represent my country in the Rugby League World Cup. 2017 has been an amazing year and I'm really looking forward to getting out to Australia and joining up with the England boys."

Daryl Powell was also delighted to see two of his players selected to pull on the England jersey: "I am absolutely delighted that two of our players are in the England World Cup squad for the tournament in Australia. Mike McMeeken has been consistently excellent in the back row for us this season and has got a great chance of cementing himself as an international player. Luke Gale has been sensational throughout the season and is already an established England international with a great opportunity to do something special with England in the World Cup."

Powell added: "I would like to wish both players and of course England all the best in the World Cup, I'm sure they will do a great job and bring the trophy home. It would certainly be fantastic for Rugby League in this country if they do."

England Head Coach Wayne Bennett said: "Selecting the final 24 with the help of my coaching staff was tough and that was down to the effort and performances of many players throughout the season. The competitiveness of Super League and NRL and knowing the goal of playing for your country in a World Cup has made many raise their game and become better athletes.

"We had to put the disappointment of the Four Nations behind us quickly and the meetings that followed that tournament set out what was required to be successful in the World Cup. Everyone has fully bought into this and we can't wait to get started."

The 24-man squad in alphabetical order (number of caps, professional and amateur clubs in brackets):

John Bateman *(6, Wigan Warriors, Bradford Dudley Hill)*

Kevin Brown *(6, Warrington Wolves, Thatto Heath Crusaders)*

Sam Burgess *(18, South Sydney Rabbitohs, Dewsbury Moor)*

Thomas Burgess *(14, South Sydney Rabbitohs, Dewsbury Moor)*

Ben Currie *(0, Warrington Wolves, Golborne Parkside)*

Luke Gale *(4, Castleford Tigers, Middleton Marauders)*

James Graham *(33, St George Illawarra Dragons, Blackbrook)*

Ryan Hall *(32, Leeds Rhinos, Oulton Raiders)*

Chris Heighington *(5, Cronulla Sharks, Umina Bunnies)*

Chris Hill *(19, Warrington Wolves, New Springs Lions)*

Josh Hodgson *(11, Canberra Raiders, East Hull)*

Jonny Lomax *(4, St Helens, Orrell St James)*

Jermaine McGillvary *(6, Huddersfield Giants, Deighton Juniors)*

Mike McMeeken *(1, Castleford Tigers, Staines Titans)*

Sean O'Loughlin *(18, Wigan Warriors, Wigan St Patricks)*

Mark Percival *(3, St Helens, Halton Farnworth Hornets)*

Stefan Ratchford *(2, Warrington Wolves, Wigan St Patricks)*

James Roby *(26, St Helens, Blackbrook)*

Scott Taylor *(2, Hull FC, Skirlaugh)*

Alex Walmsley *(0, St Helens, Dewsbury Celtic)*

Kallum Watkins *(20, Leeds Rhinos, Latchford Albion)*

Elliott Whitehead *(10, Canberra Raiders, West Bowling)*

Gareth Widdop *(21, St George Illawarra Dragons, King Cross)*

George Williams *(5, Wigan Warriors, Wigan St Patricks)*

Although it was brilliant to see both Luke and Mike get the nod by the experienced Bennett, it was also frustrating not to see Michael Shenton, Paul McShane and Greg Eden included after incredibly impressive performances for the Tigers in 2017.

#35 - Jake Trueman

Date of Birth: 16/02/1999
Country: England
Position: Scrum-Half
Previous Clubs: Bradford Bulls

Appearances: 2	**Avg. Gain:** 4.71
Tries: 3	**Tackles:** 40
Try Assists: 1	**Clean Breaks:** 1
Metres: 66	**Offloads:** 1

Jake moved to the Tigers in January 2017 from Bradford Bulls, where he had been an instrumental part of their scholarship programme and had broken into the first-team.

Despite making his debut off the bench against St Helens in June, Jake shook the Rugby League world on his full debut, scoring a hat-trick in Castleford's win at Wigan. Jake was only on the team sheet because of Luke Gale's dodgy appendix, but boy did he take advantage. An unknown quantity at the highest level, 18 years of age and playing against a team desperate to secure a top-four place, on paper it appeared as though Jake had been thrown in at the deep end without armbands. In an absolute masterclass of a performance, setting up Greg Eden's try and then recording a superb 17-minute hat-trick, the third of which he ghosted through the Wigan defence like there was nobody there, Jake announced himself on the Super League stage. It wasn't just his three tries that showcased his talent, it was how Trueman controlled the game and demonstrated remarkable composure for someone not even out of his teenage years. It was also pleasing to witness Jake complete his defensive duties with enthusiasm, regardless of his slight build, he did not take a backwards step in helping his teammates shut down Wigan attacks. It was a performance that the Castleford fans could hardly believe, but it was a performance that will live long in the memory of those supporters as well as Jake himself.

Jake went on to play the week after in the Tigers' final home game of the season. And although Castleford were on the end of a 48-16 thrashing by Hull FC, Trueman continued to impress with his accurate kicking game and his never-say-die attitude in defence. Castleford fans have to be excited about the prospect of Jake continuing to develop at the Tigers as, at just 18 years of age, he has many years ahead of him. 2018 promises to be a year where the ex-Bradford man can blossom even further.

@RichdelaRiviere – 17th September 2017: "Wow! A debut hat-trick for Jake Trueman. @GarrySchofield6 is going bananas over this kid on @rlonry!

@Oli_Holmes – 17th September 2017: "Jake Trueman, take a bow son @JT6Trueman #themessiah."

@RossWilliams_ - 17th September 2017: "Jake Trueman, eh? Always stood out when I've covered the 19s this year, but that was something else. Big future ahead. #COYF."

LARNE PATRICK LEAVES BY MUTUAL CONSENT TO JOIN LEIGH CENTURIONS ON A TWO-YEAR DEAL

Larne joined the Tigers midway through the 2016 season on an initial loan from Huddersfield Giants. He went on to secure a three-year deal at the end of 2016 that would keep him at Castleford until 2019. But after an injury-hit 2017 season where he played only seven times and failed to score, the decision was taken by mutual consent, to release Larne from his contract.

Castleford Chief Executive, Steve Gill remarked: "Larne has left the club this week and it's a decision we have come to together to benefit both the club and the player. Larne has an opportunity to play first-team football on a regular basis in the Championship and we wish him well for the next chapter of his career. I'd like to thank Larne for his time with us. Our attention is now fully focused on 2018 and I'll be 100% supporting Daryl in building the best squad possible to enter the 2018 season."

All Castleford fans wish Larne the best for the future.

JAMIE ELLIS PENS THREE-YEAR CAS DEAL

Scrum-half Jamie Ellis began his career at St Helens, but after appearing only three times in a Saints shirt moved to Championship outfit Leigh Centurions. It was at Leigh where he burst onto the scene in emphatic fashion in the 2011 season, scoring 34 tries for the Lancashire outfit who were then coached by Ian Millward. His superb form that season earned the half back a move to Super League with Hull FC for 2012. But on Humberside, he found his chances limited and a mid-season loan move saw Ellis link back up with Millward, this time at Castleford.

Ellis stayed at the club for two and a half years and was among those who appeared in the Tigers' Challenge Cup Final team in 2014. Over the course of Ellis' time at Castleford, he accrued over 200 points from just over forty games.

In 2015, Ellis moved to Huddersfield Giants where he played two seasons for the club. In this time, he notched up 47 appearances, scoring 16 tries and kicking 47 goals. In 2017, he was found surplus to requirements at the Giants by coach Rick Stone and instead helped steer Hull KR back to Super League on a one-year loan deal.

With his future up in the air at Huddersfield, it seemed likely that Ellis would once more be at Hull KR for 2018, whether on loan or permanently. However, Daryl Powell and Castleford Tigers came calling which proved too difficult for the 28-year old to resist.

Upon signing for the club, Jamie stated: "Since I've been away from Castleford I've become a bit of a fan and I've really enjoyed watching all of the success that has come to the club. I can't wait to get started and be a part of that. My agent called me while I was on holiday and told me that Castleford were interested and as soon as he said that I wanted to sign the contract to come back here."

Coach Daryl Powell spoke of the improvements that Jamie had made to his game since he moved away from the club: "I'm delighted to add Jamie Ellis to our squad for next season. He left the club a few years ago and I wanted to retain him then, his game has matured significantly since his last time at Castleford and I am confident he will be outstanding for us alongside Luke Gale and give us a great combination at half back. He has many attributes to his game, his passing ability and running games alongside a very long kicking ability will add-to our armoury for 2018."

MITCH CLARK SIGNS FOR CASTLEFORD ON A TWO-YEAR DEAL

Son of former Leeds, Bradford Northern and Featherstone hooker, Trevor Clark, and born in Pontefract, Mitch Clark began his career with Australian club Penrith Panthers and was a vital figure in their under-20s' Holden Cup Grand Final victory in 2013.

From Penrith, he made his move to Doncaster for the 2015 season where he appeared 23 times for the South Yorkshire club. After impressive performances, he secured a deal at Bradford Bulls ahead of the 2016 season and went on to play 24 games in a Bulls' shirt. But with the club's liquidation in early 2017, he was on the move again, this time to Hull KR where he played 15 games in the Robins' promotion-chasing season.

Clark has again decided to move on and found joining the Tigers too good an opportunity to turn down: "I can't wait to rip into pre-season. I was born in Pontefract and to get to play for this club and to play for Daryl Powell is such a massive opportunity for me. I just can't wait to get started!"

Daryl Powell was delighted to secure a player who he has had his eye on for a while: "Mitch Clark is a player I have known for a long time having discussed his future with him three years ago. I'm delighted he has signed for Castleford at this time as I believe he has a big future with us. He is an all-action front rower who has great leg speed when carrying the ball and real intent when he is defending. I welcome Mitch to the club and look forward to working with him."

CASTLEFORD ENTER INTO A DUAL-REGISTRATION AGREEMENT WITH HALIFAX RLFC

This agreement with Halifax will replace the one with Batley Bulldogs which saw a number of Tigers players gain valuable playing time at the Fox's Biscuits Stadium in the past two years. Notably, current first-team player and young starlet, Greg Minikin played 7 games for the Bulldogs in 2016 before establishing himself in the Castleford first team.

Halifax themselves have been one of the top performing Championship sides for a number of years, and despite them being only part-time, they have finished in the top four in two of the past three seasons. The two clubs already have a link in the shape of Tigers youngster Brandon Douglas who spent much of 2017 on loan at Fax, making 11 appearances for the club.

Castleford coach Daryl Powell believed that the agreement would benefit both clubs: "I'm delighted that we have reached an agreement on dual registration with Halifax Rugby League club. I worked with Richard Marshall over the course of the season when Brandon Douglas was playing there and only have positive things to say about how he works. Dual registration is an important part of player development at the moment. We have a number of players who will play at Halifax to benefit both Halifax and the players themselves over the course of the season. I look forward to this relationship be an outstanding one for both Castleford and Halifax."

Tigers CEO, Steve Gill was also enthusiastic about the two clubs coming together: "We welcome the opportunity to link up with Halifax RLFC as our Dual Registration partners. Both Daryl Powell and Richard Marshall are looking forward to sharing ideas and practices with each other, which should be beneficial for all players and coaches. Dual Registration does have its complications but we are looking forward to working alongside Halifax in 2018 and beyond."

Gill also praised Castleford's previous dual-registration partner, Batley, for how well they had conducted themselves in the past two years: "Although we will not be dual registering with the Batley Bulldogs next year, I would like to thank them for their honesty and integrity as a club, and we will continue to work with them should the chance arise."

Halifax CEO Mark Moore also expressed excitement at the agreement: "We see the relationship with Castleford Tigers as a statement of intent, both in respect of the style of play, which will excite our fans and the high quality of the players available. There will be opportunities for our own youngsters in the Tigers' Junior sides, and for Tigers Players with our reserves. This is very much a partnership in player development."

Conclusion

2017 cannot be described as anything but a remarkable breakthrough season for Castleford Tigers. The performances, excitement and publicity that Castleford Tigers generated, the 2017 season will live long in the memory of all those associated with the club.

With just seven losses from 34 competitive matches, a League Leaders' Shield in their cabinet and a Grand Final appearance, six Dream Team nominees and the Man of Steel and Rugby League Writers' Player of the Year in their ranks, having received the Club of the Year and with the Coach of the Year leading the team, being the highest points scorers with the top try scorer in the league on the wing, and ending the regular season and Super 8s top, for the first in Castleford's 91-year history, with a record ten points separating the club and their nearest rivals with a 300-plus points average, Castleford Tigers announced themselves onto the scene in 2017 like no other team in history.

The Tigers experienced Old Trafford for the first time in the Super League era and, though the end result was painful, it was perhaps a vital learning curve for 17 players that had just one Grand Final appearance between them (Michael Shenton). The intense feeling of disappointment amongst the fans and the whole club is still very raw. But on reflection, this frustration, if channelled correctly, can drive the standards of the players wearing the Castleford Tigers jersey even higher and can propel the team to even greater success in 2018.

The saying "you've got to lose one to win one" may be dismissed so soon after the showpiece event, but it is something to hold on to at least for Castleford fans still hurting. Daryl Powell looked visibly distressed in his post-match interview, whilst the players appeared incredibly sullen and even embarrassed after the Grand Final performance. It is an experience that no coach or player wants to go through in Rugby League.

But, just ten years ago, this fantastic and extraordinary club had yet again secured their Super League status with a victory over Widnes Vikings in the winner-takes-all play-off at Headingley. The average Tigers fan has over the years just wanted a team of which they could be proud. To have witnessed the transformation of a team who were fighting for their lives in the 2007 Championship Grand Final to a team fighting for the right to be crowned champions in the 2017 Super League Grand Final was, for almost every Castleford fan, a dream come true.

It is no surprise then, on the back of such a wondrous season, that Castleford Tigers are the bookies' favourites to win the Grand Final next October. The remarkable 2017 was a testament to the work that Daryl Powell, his coaching staff and the players have put in in the past few years. With the coaching staff and vital players all signed up for years to come, the future, as the bookies predict, appears promising. And one can be assured that the club will not rest on their laurels; the 2018 season is just a few months away.

No one can really predict the outcome of next year, but as every season tends to be for a Castleford fan, 2018 promises to be one hell of a ride. Here's to a previously unthinkable 2017 and hopefully, a 2018 that can see Castleford go one step further.

You might also like

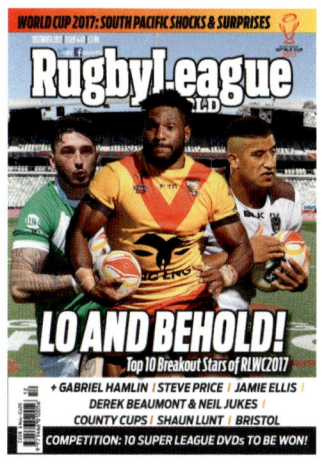

Rugby League World

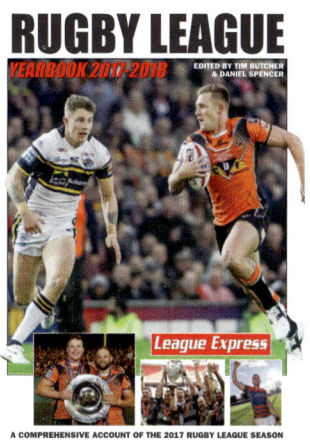

Rugby League Yearbook

Rugby Leaguer & League Express

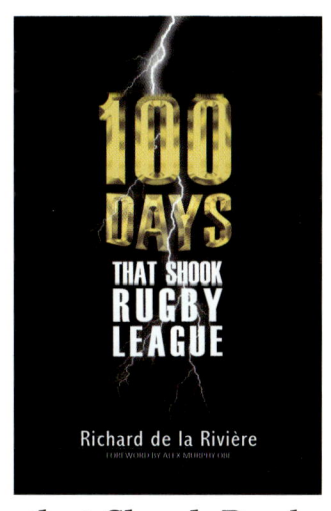

100 Days that Shook Rugby League

totalrl.com/shop